Will
The Real Me
Please
Stand Up?

D1125421

Will
The Real Me
Please
Stand Up?

Jeanette C. Zweifel, Ed.D

Illustrated by
Susan Breck Smith

Nell Thurber Press

Nell Thurber Press
61 Swift Lane
Naperville, IL 60565
630.355.3367

Printed in the United States of America
on acid free paper

ISBN: 0-9722364-0-6

Library of Congress Cataloging-in-Publication Data
Zweifel, Jeanette C.
    Will the real me please stand up?

    Includes index and bibliography

LCCN : 2002093908

Illustrated by Susan Breck Smith • Cover design by Nina Davis

To Ken...

Do I contradict myself?
Very well then I contradict myself,
(I am large, I contain multitudes.)

Walt Whitman
Song of Myself

TABLE OF CONTENTS

PREFACE

In 1979 I was a new doctoral student standing in awe of my professor Betty Bosdell, Ph.D. The ideas I was learning were new and exciting and definitely scary! Betty had a way of name-dropping, as if you knew who she was talking about. The safest modus operandi was to stand and wait. Hopefully she would eventually say something that would connect and you would (more or less) figure out to whom she was referring. And so, on a memorable occasion she announced, "The Yeomans are coming, the Yeomans are coming!" Those of us who stood in awe, nodded with what we prayed was a knowing look on our faces and waited. We finally discovered that the "Yeomans" were not a long-lost tribe or invaders from the deep. They were a couple who worked with a theory called psychosynthesis and Betty was very excited about this theory. She had been studying with Ann and Tom Yeomans and other psychosynthesis practitioners for some time and wanted to turn on her students to these exciting ideas.

New to the doctoral program, I responded to her call with trepidation. I did screw up my courage and invited my friend and mentor, Helen Haugsnes, to join me to hear the "Yeomans." I was hooked after hearing the presentation and processing it with Helen. From this introductory evening, I progressed to Betty's advanced classes in psychosynthesis, to assisting her in teaching the psychosynthesis courses, to monthly psychosynthesis gatherings at her home, to teaching therapists on a private basis with her after her retirement. A synthesizing experience was when I attended an international psychosynthesis conference in Toronto with Betty.

Needless to say, when Betty said "Carolyn Conger is coming!" and "Hal and Sidra are coming!" I no longer waited—I just signed up! I learned Voice Dialogue from Hal and Sidra Stone at Betty's urging and continued to learn and study and practice under Betty's tutelage. It is from all of these experiences that I became proficient in working with the concept of "subpersonalities," or parts of the self. As I worked with my own parts, I learned that I could do the dialogue on paper with amazing results. That is what I have set out to teach the readers of this book.

This book has had a number of wonderful guinea pigs: my clients, students who signed on for a class and convinced me to entitle my book the same as the title of the class, and some others who were intrigued and wanted to try it out. Their feedback has been invaluable. They rallied to "I'm writing a book!" as I rallied to "The Yeomans are coming!"

There have been many exceptional teachers in my life and I have been gifted by their presence. Probably everything I write comes from them, with some twists that I hope are uniquely my own. Psychosynthesis grounded me in theory and formed the foundation from which all the rest comes.

Hal and Sidra Stone have written *the* books on Voice Dialogue and you will find them listed among the references. This powerful and unique way of working with subpersonalities is theirs and I have learned enormously from every encounter with them.

Carolyn Conger has been an inspiration and great teacher for twenty years, expanding on ideas of spirit and dreams and connectedness. While coming from a different framework, my consultant and therapist, John Hofstra, has taught me about gentleness of spirit, inclusiveness, and being safe to grow beyond my original story. Betty has been my source, my nudge, my teacher, and my mentor. My clients, interns, students, and supervisees have provided an opportunity for me to teach and learn from their learning.

What appears on the following pages has evolved from all of these people, their work and their spirit. Those who read and "work the work," will become members of this community of learning and growth and spirit. I invite you and welcome you.

Jeanette C. Zweifel, Ed.D.

Chapter 1
GETTING ACQUAINTED

You have just opened a book entitled, *Will the Real Me Please Stand Up?* I wish I could ask you what made you open it. When I taught my first class on this topic, some students told me the title was what made them sign up. Others said it was the description that promised to give them tools to recognize the "selves within the self" and break through barriers that would free them to resolve life dilemmas and move forward.

We are going on a journey together. I hope that it will be a fun and fascinating journey for you and that it will result in a sense of greater self-knowledge and acceptance. I am going to be talking to you as if you were right here with me. I hope you will talk back, even though I can't hear you. We'll be breaking ground together in a novel way of internal communication so why not pretend we are talking to each other as well?

The only thing I know about you is that you picked up this book. The only things you know about me are what is on the cover or in the preface. I will be sharing some of my personal self along the way. I hope you will, too. I won't hear you but you will hear yourself. There will be lots of dialogue but it will all be among your "selves." And very likely, somewhere along the way, things will begin to shift for you. You will begin to see changes that will excite you. Events you felt uncertain about will turn out wonderfully. You will make decisions you've been sitting on the fence about for a long time. Or you will find yourself venturing into areas that once held hesitancy or even trepidation for you.

In this first chapter, the concept of "parts" of the personality will be explained. Examples will be used to help make the concept more clear and applicable. Hopefully, it will help you get started thinking in terms of parts of yourself.

The Basic Concept

Did you ever say "There is a part of me that...?" Often, when we can't make a decision, or know what we *should* do, we use this language to explain our feeling of being stuck, unable to take action. Without even knowing it, we are acknowledging that we have different parts that have different ideas about what is good for us. The idea of parts of the personality is so much a part of the common vernacular that we don't even realize it represents a psychological framework. In this book you will be given some tools to recognize the "selves within the self." We are not looking at pathology or disease. If your mother told you it is crazy to talk to yourself, or like mine, that it is okay to talk to yourself as long as you don't answer, she was wrong. It is not crazy. It is normal. It is even healthy. We are going to expand on the whole idea of talking to yourself—and answering! We're going to give it a structure and see how it can help you to work out dilemmas in your life and better understand your inner workings.

This may sound a bit far fetched but I would like to invite you to approach this whole concept with a "beginner's mind." This means to suspend judgment and go with the flow for awhile. Let your mind take these ideas as if you are "beginning" instead of measuring every idea against what you already know. For the next few minutes, try to have a beginner's mind. Before long we will check in and see how you are doing. You will know if it isn't making sense in your own belief system and then you can jump ship if you like.

You may be asking, "So, why is it we would do this—think of ourselves in terms of parts?" That is a good question. Let's try a few examples of circumstances where this way of approaching your own personality can be helpful.

So back to that time when you said to yourself or out loud, "There's a part of me...?" Maybe you couldn't decide whether to paint your room blue or terra cotta. While telling a friend about your indecision you said, "A part of me loves the cool, quietness of blue. It reminds me of the lake or a clear summer sky. But a part of me loves the earthy feel of terra cotta. It makes me think of Arizona and sun-baked landscapes."

Often when we are faced with a dilemma, large or small, we think and speak in terms of parts. Until now you may not have been aware of doing this. Pay attention for the next few days to your own language and to that of friends or even newscasters. You will catch people saying "a part of me." It is often related to a dilemma. The speaker is ascribing opposing points of view to separate parts of the personality.

Using the room color question, imagine that it was your dilemma and I asked you, "What do you know about the part of you that likes blue?" If this is a whole new way of looking at things it will feel a little strange. But let's pretend it is your dilemma and you know you do have a part that would be voting for blue. In answer to this question you might say, "Well, that is the part of me that likes quiet and serenity. It is the part that loves to sit alone by the lake on a quiet day and contemplate the universe. The blue sky and blue water make me feel serene and peaceful. This part of me would want to paint the room blue because it would bring about that memory and that feeling."

Then I would say, "And what do you know about the part of you that prefers terra cotta?" You might answer, "That is my creative part! It loves bold, earthy colors. It feels inspired by the landscapes of Arizona and it makes me want to paint, or work with clay. It definitely wants the room painted terra cotta so I can put myself in the Arizona frame of mind and feel the creative juices flow."

Even though it may sound a little silly, can you see how this further explains the dilemma? Now you have reasons why you feel stuck. There are two opposing points of view—all within *you*. You might use this new information to help you decide. If you know you want this room for quiet reflection, the first part would win the argument. If you know you want it for creativity, it would be the second. If I were there asking, and you said you still felt stuck, I'd ask "What other parts of you may have an opinion about this?" You will see more of how this might work out later when I use this dilemma to give a sample dialogue.

Another cause for being stuck may be fear. Sometimes we don't even know we are afraid, we just aren't moving or we are feeling uneasy in an ill-defined way. The uneasiness might be stopping us from doing what we want or just making us uncomfortable. Working with our parts can help us understand what is really going on. My friend, Sally, has given me permission to explain how this worked for her.

Sally has a beautiful singing voice. For many years she had not been performing except in church. Some years ago, she was encouraged by a friend to send an audition tape to a well-known summer music festival. Sally thought it might be fun to sing in the chorus of an opera, so she sent the tape. To her surprise, delight, and trepidation she was given a part in the opera—not the chorus but a significant role! A few weeks before she left for the rehearsals, she attended a workshop I was leading and volunteered to be the subject in a demonstration of parts work.

As the subject, Sally shared her excitement and uneasiness. She talked about feeling inadequate and nervous about working with seasoned professionals when she felt like an amateur. As we began talking in parts language, she identified a part that was afraid. That part told us she was only four years old and was terrified of going out on stage. We acknowledged how scary it would be for a four year old to go out there with all those grown ups. I suggested maybe Sally could leave her backstage. This little one could have the fun of watching and being part of the excitement but she wouldn't have to perform. The grown-up performer part of Sally could do the singing and acting. That part was excited about being out there with the seasoned performers.

Sally reported feeling much calmer about the opera performance and later told me she had a wonderful time, never feeling the shaking fear of the four year old.

These examples are two uses of the parts concept: the first helps to resolve indecision; the second to recognize and resolve fear that seems to be irrational and unexplainable. It takes practice and lots more understanding to use this (that's why we don't stop here but have a whole book ahead of us!) I use this technique in my work as a therapist to help clients gain self-understanding and get unstuck. I use it in my own life, through a journaling technique I am going to teach you here.

TAKING STOCK

Take a moment to check in with yourself. What are you feeling about the ideas in the first section? If you think it sounds like some weirdo is at the keyboard you might want to stop now. If you are a little skeptical but still interested, keep reading. Can everyone do this? Probably. But not everyone wants to. People who are very logical and for whom intuition seems like a foreign culture, sometimes find this work frustrating. My engineer/computer scientist husband says, "Why can't you just make two lists—the pros and the cons, compare and analyze them and come up with an answer?" You can. If that sounds good to you, go for it! If you say, "Well...Yeah...But I've done that and I still can't decide what feels right," maybe this book is for you.

That word "feels" in the sentence above is important. This is an intuitive process. If you always make decisions based on reasoning, you may be like my husband and not like this approach.

On the other hand, if you often decide by "feeling" your way, this approach is likely right up your alley. If you are intrigued but know you are one of those logical guys/gals, don't quit yet. I've had engineers and accountants like this, too. After all, we all use *both* sides of our brains— the right side which is more intuitive and the left which is more logical. Sometimes the challenge and the fun in learning something new is enhanced when it tickles the side of our brain we feel less at home in.

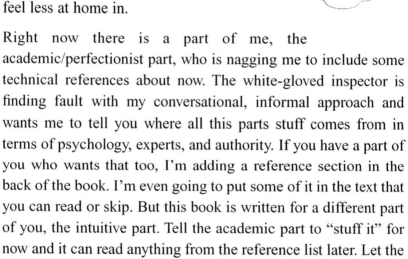

Right now there is a part of me, the academic/perfectionist part, who is nagging me to include some technical references about now. The white-gloved inspector is finding fault with my conversational, informal approach and wants me to tell you where all this parts stuff comes from in terms of psychology, experts, and authority. If you have a part of you who wants that too, I'm adding a reference section in the back of the book. I'm even going to put some of it in the text that you can read or skip. But this book is written for a different part of you, the intuitive part. Tell the academic part to "stuff it" for now and it can read anything from the reference list later. Let the part of you that loves to play, to explore new ideas, to stretch and grow read on.

Now we are going to begin doing some journal work. The second chapter helps you begin to identify your own parts, learn how to expand on you understanding of them, and tap into your intuition.

Chapter 2
GETTING STARTED

We are going to be learning to use journaling to work with our parts. So you will need to get a journal. I recommend one with at least six by nine inch pages. Choose your journal with your intuition. Hold it in your hand. Feel its heft. Do you like the feel of it? Do lines appeal or feel restrictive? Is a spiral binding more comfortable or do you like something bound? Allow yourself to have what you like. Now you need a good pen that moves easily across the page. It should write at a speed that feels comfortable to you and have a tone and color that resonate with you.

Journal and pen at the ready, we shall begin the work. The working sections will be called "sessions" because in therapy that is what the time spent with a therapist is called. In this case, you are doing your own therapy. When you see "session," you will know it is time to grab your journal and pen or get ready for an exercise where you will close your eyes and work in your imagination. Working in your imagination by following suggestions is called "guided imagery." In our work together, I will be making the suggestions. You are always free to improvise and even go off on your own.

SESSION ONE—TWO PARTS

In a moment we are going to crack open that nice, new journal and *write* something in it. Are you one of those people (like I am, sometimes) who hates to mess up those beautiful, pristine pages? Do you have a part of you that wants to make it perfect (oh, we are going to hear more about *that* part, believe me!)? Let's make a deal. Tell all of your parts something for me. Tell them that this journal is for you to *play* in! It is not going to be perfect because you are learning something new. Nothing you write in it is written with a chisel in stone. It is written with ordinary ink on plain old paper (even if it is in a pretty journal). You can scratch things out. You can even tear out whole pages if you want. Or you can let everything be and recognize that it is just what came to you in that moment. A minute later, you could decide it is something else and then you can write *that*. This journal is a fluid work in progress—let go, let it flow, and reserve judgment (yes, a little later we'll hear more about the part that criticizes, too!)

We are going to begin with a question or a dilemma and see if we can identify two parts of you that have something to say about it. Sometimes beginners try to take on too much. If you picked up this book because you have a big issue in your life that you are trying to resolve and you thought this might help, it probably will. But not yet. To begin, choose something simple to contemplate. Choose a dilemma or question that is not going to determine the course of the rest of your life. Even whether to paint that room blue or terra cotta or what couch to buy might be too big. Maybe you could just ask, "What do I know about the part of me that picked up this book?" or "Shall I choose to go camping for the weekend or to that concert Saturday night?" We'll use the latter question as an example. As long as your question doesn't strike fear in your heart or make your hand tremble, it is probably okay!

In your journal write this question, "What do I know about the part of me that wants [to go to the concert]?" (Insert in the brackets whatever fits your chosen question). Trust whatever flows off the end of your pen in response to this question. Try to be an objective recorder. If your language takes on a severe tone, your inner critic part might be doing the writing. Step back for a moment. Ask: "Who is writing?" If it feels like a critic, ask that part to step aside and call up a part that *can* be an objective recorder. If your critic is particularly strong and digs in, try telling it you understand it wants to keep you on track. But for right now you want to try this new thing. No one has to read this stuff. You'll let the critic talk later. This is a private experiment.

Principle: Every part has a positive intent; therefore, every part must be honored. (Yes, even the Critic!)

Now ask "Who holds the opposite point of view?" [Who wants to go camping?] What do you know about this part? Again allow whatever comes to find its way to the page. Do not censor your writing. This is for you. Nothing is written in stone for time immemorial. It is all fluid. What is true in this moment may be discarded later. There will be time to review and cull the wheat from the chaff. Trust yourself and allow whatever comes.

If we follow through with the questions in our example about the concert and the camping weekend, our work might look like this:

What do I know about the part of me that wants to go camping? This is my adventurous, outdoor part. It is the part of me that loves to be in nature, to hike, to be away from the hectic pace of my life. This part loves the smell of the woods, the quiet, the slower pace.

What do I know about the part of me that wants to go to the concert? This part of me is kind of refined. It likes culture. It especially loves good music. This is the part of me that calls a friend and suggests an evening of a quiet dinner and a concert. It is a sociable part but it likes to experience entertainment rather than go to a party or have a chatty evening.

Do you have two distinct parts now? Close your eyes. Do you have a sense of each part? Maybe you can "see" each one. Sometimes it is easier at first to use your hands and imagine feeling the part. Or listening to the sounds/words of the part. It may even have a smell. Use the sense that is most available to you to get the clearest idea of each part. If you are not a visual learner/perceiver, experiment with your other senses to find the modality that gives you easiest access. I will be speaking in terms of the visual because it is accessed by many of us. It is not *better* to "see." So feel free to translate my instructions into your most accessible sense. [If you are unsure about all this, try *Exercise I: The Apple* on page 130 in the Appendix section. It will help you discover your strongest sense.]

Let's flesh out these two parts even more. In your journal, make note of everything you are aware of about each part. Use your imagination. Try not to censor what comes to you. You might be surprised to discover a part is not the same gender as you. This is not cause for alarm. Most of us have some opposite gender parts. Notice the following about each part:

- **How it is dressed**
- **How old it appears to be**
- **Its gender**
- **Its carriage**
- **Its size**
- **Its demeanor**

In our example we might write the following:

I can see my adventurous part. It is male. He is dressed in khaki with hiking boots, a fisherman's hat, and a walking stick. He is tanned and wears sun glasses. He is my age and is fit and enthusiastic about being active. He loves to set up camp and go exploring a new wooded area.

My concert lover is female. She is soft and refined looking. She wears a nice longish skirt and a soft, wool blazer with a silk scarf and gold earrings. She, too, is my age. She wears her hair pulled back in a neat style and has a quiet voice. She chooses friends who enjoy the same kind of music she likes and can spend an evening listening without much conversation. She looks well put together.

Use some colored pencils, crayons, or other art materials and see if you can get a representation of each part on the page. It may be represented by a color, a shape, a symbol, or look like a person (stick figures are fine). Allowing ourselves to use different media, sometimes accesses more from the unconscious. Suspend judgment. Whatever shows up is what is supposed to be there for now.

Does a name occur to you for each part? Sometimes parts are called by something related to their function: The Critic, The Perfectionist, The Angry One. Sometimes metaphorical names come to us: The Bear, The Wolf, The Giant. Most of us have a Vulnerable Child and a Playful Child. These parts might have names that you were called as a child. A five-year old part of me is called, Jeanie. That is what I was called when I was five. Don't think too much about names, let them emerge. If nothing comes, just label them Part 1 and Part 2 for now. Later, when we learn to dialogue with the parts, you might ask each one what it wants to be called.

Example:

The part that wants to go camping is called Ed the Explorer. The concert goer is called Sophisticated Lady.

TAKING STOCK

Have you got one or two pages in your journal filled by now? Maybe you have six! Flip through the pages and notice how it feels to look at them. Don't read it yet. Just "feel" it. This is an intuitive process. We are practicing allowing ourselves to feel and to trust what emerges.

What? Your pages are blank? Do not panic. Take a moment to check in with yourself. Do you feel this is totally alien material? Are you excited but feeling inadequate? Do you still *want* it to work for you? It is okay to revert to making lists. But if you still want to do this, don't give up. Take a deep breath. Say, "I can allow this to happen. My intuition functions. I can take my time and allow whatever comes to come." Begin at the beginning. If things don't begin to come, there are exercises in the Appendix that will help you. Try The Bus (p. 133), The Room (p. 135), or

The Pie (p. 136). Depending on your frustration level right now, decide whether you need to take a break. Be gentle with yourself.

If you have something on your pages, trust that it is exactly what is supposed to be there. This is sometimes hard. Later, we will talk more about why it is so hard. For now, accept that it is not always easy. Try not to compare your work with the work of anyone else who is doing this. We will continue to give ourselves lots of latitude as we work. It helps to use affirmative statements to counter critical voices. Say things like: "What I have written is exactly what I am supposed to do in this moment. I can do this work. It is okay to allow whatever emerges. I can make sense out of it later." [By the way, if you follow this instruction, you are now officially talking to yourself!]

Review the work on your pages and make note of anything that seems important to you. Keep notes brief so you don't get bogged down in detail. You just need enough to remind yourself of what thoughts came to you.

We will move onto letting the parts talk in Chapter 3. Some examples will demonstrate how dialogue works, how to get past blocks, and what questions to ask.

Chapter 3
DIALOGUE

Dialogue is truly the name of the game. Our goal is to talk to the parts through this process called dialogue. The dialogue is how we get to know the parts and what each part wants and needs. If you don't feel confident you have identified two parts, read on— I think it will begin to make sense and you might be surprised by what shows up on your pages. Sometimes the magic happens when we start the pen moving across the page.

SESSION TWO—BEGINNING DIALOGUE

When you write dialogue, think of it in a play-writer's format. It then looks like a script. You will have the name of each part (even if it is Part 1 and Part 2) at the beginning of its speech. You might want to choose a letter or symbol to represent the one asking the questions. In the last chapter when we wrote "What do I know about the part..." someone was asking the question. Usually that will be "you," the centered self, the ego. I simply use my first name initial, "J." I'll refer to this part as the self or "s" for demonstration purposes.

Allow enough time in this one sitting to have each part speak. This is very important.

Principle: Allowing a part to express itself strengthens it and gives it energy.

If you allow only one part to speak, you will make that subpersonality more present in your life and you may feel unbalanced. If a negative part gets the floor, it is especially important to balance that energy with the other side. Most parts have an opposite, their polarity. While every part has a positive intent, its behavior in our lives is not always positive. As we work, we want to keep the idea of balance in mind.

In our example, we will begin by having the self (s) ask Ed the Explorer (or EE as we will refer to him) a question:

self (s): *EE, will you tell me more about you?*

Ed (EE): *I am the part of you that loves the outdoors and exploring. I don't like to sit in stuffy concert halls or wear all that prissy stuff—like skirts and blazers, silk scarves, and gold earrings! I like to be on the move and doing active things. I am the one who bought a trail bike and who says lets get some roller blades. When you were little, I was the tom boy in you. Maybe I still am!*

s: *Thanks, EE. It is good to hear from you. I like the energy you bring to my life. You help me get exercise and interesting adventures. You are fun. Do you feel you have enough air time in my life?*

EE: *NO! You spend way too much time dressed up, working, and going to concerts and quiet dinners and movies!*

s: *What would you do if you had more air time in my life?*

Explorer Ed

Sophisticated Lady

EE: *I'd go places a lot more. We would use that mountain bike I bought and you parked in the garage— every weekend. And we would plan lots more camping trips. Remember wanting to go to the Grand Canyon and Yosemite to camp? That's me! Let's go! You'd have a lot more fun and be much more fit if you let me run things!*

s: *I know you are right. I will try to pay more attention to you and find more time to do what you like. Now, Sophisticated Lady (SL from now on) what about you?*

SL: *I love concerts. I like to be with friends who like good music and don't have to talk all the time. I like to dress in an understated sort of dressy. It makes me feel good to have good clothes. I like things neat and well ordered and pretty quiet.*

s: *It is good to know you, too. I like your taste. I think you show up when I need you like at meetings at work.*

SL: *Yes, I am the part of you that dresses for the meeting and shakes hands and makes nice.*

s: *Do you talk at the meeting?*

SL: *Yes, if things are organized and orderly and pleasant. But some other part of you comes in to handle things if you need to get tough.*

s: *Yes, I think I know who that is. Do you feel like you get enough air time in my life?*

SL: *Usually. I don't like it when you want to be a slob and lay around the house in your sweats. I'm not against the explorer guy but his ideas of fun aren't mine. You usually let me have enough time.*

Are you beginning to get the idea? Start writing. Keep your pen moving across the page. Don't edit. Most of us have a part that criticizes us, The Critic. Don't let the Critic get involved if you can help it. If you feel your Critic is complaining about what you are writing, you may need to stop and ask "Critic, do you want to talk?" If this happens, continue the dialogue with the Critic or whatever part of you emerges (maybe it won't be the Critic—a scared part perhaps). Ask the intruding part, "What is going on for you? What about this process concerns you? What do you need to make it okay for me to proceed? How can I help you?" Remember the principle "Honor each part."

Continuing the above example:

Critic (C): *This is stupid! You aren't doing it right. Why do you keep asking if the part that is talking has enough air time? It is talking isn't it? I think you have it all wrong.*

self (s): *Ah, Critic. I see you are not taking this lying down.*

C: *Why should I? You never do anything right. I'm sure you don't understand the directions. You better find someone to ask and see how it is supposed to be done.*

s: *Critic, I understand these directions. Over and over we are being told there is not a wrong way to do this. What do you need to make it okay to proceed?*

C: *I guess just to know you are paying attention.*

s: *Do you know that I am smart enough to understand this?*

C: *Yeah, I guess so. I just get nervous when you barge ahead and do this "let the pen move across the page" thing. It feels like you are not paying attention and that you are bound to get it wrong. You make a lot of mistakes, you know!*

s: *Yes. I guess that is how I learn. But I do learn. Will you try to stay back and let me try this out?*

C: *I guess. We'll see how it goes.*

Some good questions for "s" to ask any part:

- **What is your job in my life?**
- **How old are you?**
- **What do you want?**
- **What do you need?**
- **Do you get enough air time?**
- **If you had more air time what would you do?**
- **What do you think needs to happen?**
- **What do you know about Part 2?**

Sometimes people think all of their parts are the same age as they are. However, most of us have parts that are different ages. The parts evolve to deal with things going on in our lives beginning at a very early age. (This is further explained early in the next chapter). It makes sense that some of them would be the age you were when they evolved. So don't be surprised if a child or teenager shows up! If your part is young, remember to keep your questions simple. If you are talking to a 6 year old, you cannot ask sophisticated questions and expect to get answers! When it feels like the conversation is complete, thank the part and tell it you would like to hear from it again sometime. If you run out of time before it feels finished, promise to come back soon.

Going back to the example with EE and SL, the writer here learns that there is some imbalance in her life. The EE part wants more air time and has good things to offer. SL gets enough. This gives her information she can use if she chooses to do so.

TAKING STOCK

Now you are officially talking to yourself *and* answering! [Sorry, Mom.] How are you feeling? A little silly? That's to be expected. You will get used to it. Are you beginning to find the pen has a life of its own? Are you able to trust whatever comes, even if it does not make a lot of sense to you right now? Does it seem like a struggle and only a few sentences emerge? Is the dialogue a bit strained and stilted? All of these are normal. This work takes practice and you are just beginning. Let your Cheerleader (or the part of you that encourages you and pats you on the back) have a few moments of your time.

To further our understanding of this concept of parts, we will next explore the difference between parts and roles. We'll talk more about the uses of the parts model and where parts come from. We will list some parts that many of us have in common and relate the idea to Carl Jung's model of archetypes. You will get all of the parts of yourself that you have identified so far on a list.

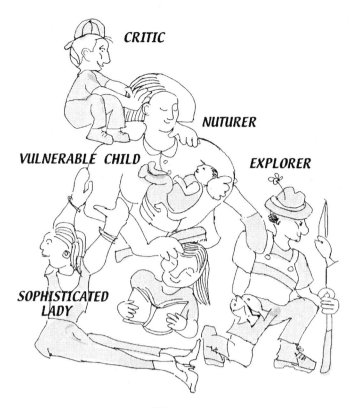

CRITIC

NUTURER

VULNERABLE CHILD

EXPLORER

SOPHISTICATED
LADY

Chapter 4
MORE ABOUT PARTS

You are probably beginning to have a good sense about this parts thing. Sometimes we call the parts "subpersonalities." Sometimes they are called "energies." I will use these terms interchangeably from now on. More than one name for something can make it easier to comprehend.

People will sometimes say, "Oh, I know what you mean. You are talking about roles." If you noticed, I did not include the term "roles" in my list of alternative names. That is because the idea of role is related but doesn't quite define this concept of subpersonalities. A role is function. When you pick the kids up at soccer practice, you are performing the role of "mom." If you are at work you might say, "I am in the role of worker." However, in either of these roles, any one of your subpersonalities might be operating. If you yell at the kids for dragging mud into the car, it might be your Critic or the Slave who is talking. If your work is going great and you have just completed something important with great ingenuity, it may be your Creative Part or the Artist that has been present in the role of worker. "Mom" is a role in which your Nurturing Part probably gets to come out often.

Are you wondering where the parts come from or why they are present? Imagine a baby coming into the world and being impacted in many ways. This new, vulnerable personality must find ways to cope and get needs met. As the world impacts on the personality, the parts develop as a way of coping and taking care of the "self." If you watch young children closely you can see that the parts emerge at a very early age. Perhaps because I am so attuned to this way of thinking, I feel I could see parts in my grandchildren when they were six months old. One child has a strong cautious part that watches, observes, considers before acting. That same child has a part that is totally invested in an activity once committed. As the children develop, the parts of their personalities become more evident.

And why again are we choosing to look at our "selves" in this way? One reason is that it can help us resolve dilemmas. But a more important reason is that it can help us become more inte- grated, feel more balanced, and decrease self-destructive behav- iors. It can also help us access parts that have not been very active in our lives but that have valuable things to offer. You may discover you have a creative part that was shut down very early in your life but can make lovely pictures, beautiful music, or write wonderful stories. You probably have a nurturing subper- sonality that can help a child part feel cared for and loved. But maybe that nurturing part has not had much opportunity to act on your behalf. Perhaps you tend to spend most of your time in a feeling energy but can access a thinking part who can help you make decisions.

Think of the personality as an orchestra. The players in an orchestra tune their instruments and practice while they are waiting for a performance to begin. This basically sounds like discordant noise. But when the conductor raises the baton and begins the concert, all the parts of the orchestra work together and create beautiful music. The conductor has to know all the parts of the music  they are playing and often is able to play many of the instruments. In this work, we are trying to become the conductors of our own orchestras so that we can create harmony rather than discordance. To do that, we have to learn all the parts of our music.

There are many similarities in the parts each person will identify. The famous psychologist, Carl Jung, talked about archetypes. These are universal personality parts. For example, we might imagine that most people have a Warrior part of them—a part that fights, or would fight, for survival or an ideal. In some people, the Warrior is very strong and plays a large role in the personality. In others, this is a fairly inactive part. But most of us can recognize that energy. This is an archetype. [If that academic part of you is screaming for more about this, look in the reference section.]

Some common subpersonalities are: The Critic, The Child (may be divided into Vulnerable Child and Playful Child), The Perfectionist, The Controller/Protector, The Scared One, The Angry One, and The Pusher. There are more in this list but you get the idea. You may be thinking, "Yes, I have one of each!" Don't limit your list to this one or these particular names. You will find that other names occur to you for these parts. Use the names that your parts want to be called. For demonstration purposes, I will use these functional kinds of names because I think then we will all know what we are talking about.

SESSION THREE—THE PLAYERS SO FAR

In the last session, you identified two parts and let each of them talk to you. As you have read more about the subpersonalities, have you been saying to yourself, "Oh, I think I have a part that...?" I hope you have already begun to identify some others besides the first two. Start a list of the parts you know you have. When you look at my suggestions in the paragraph before this one where I talk about the parts that many people have, be sure you individualize these parts to reflect the unique you. As you make your list, go inside and just reflect for a moment. Ask yourself, "Who else is there?" Your list will not be complete now—or ever. This is a work in progress, remember. We never know all there is to know. If your list is very short, don't worry—more will come to you later. If it is very long, look at it and see if it seems like some of the parts may be sub-parts of another—perhaps you need to group some together.

Don't fall into the trap of being judgmental about your list. It is fine the way it is. If it has 20 subpersonalities on it and that feels right to you—leave it. If some of them belong together, there will come a time in this work when they will let you know. If you only have the two parts we started with, that is all right, too. Soon we are going to work together to ferret out another part.

Before you move on, you might want to get out your art materials and draw the parts on your list. Drawing is another way of getting more information from the unconscious. There are no rules about art work. Let yourself imagine the part and put on your paper whatever comes. Sometimes you will get a symbol instead of a person. Trust that and let it be. Later you will see a diagram that is a map of parts and one person's interpretation of the map. Her drawing uses symbols and words to depict the parts.

TAKING STOCK

How are you doing? Are we having fun yet? Do you feel some resistance to making a list or to doing any of the work suggested? I am not sure I understand why this is but it seems our unconscious is often very reluctant to turn over its treasures. When we set out to elicit unknown material, there seems to be a reluctance to sit down and *do* it. If you find that this is true for you, simply acknowledge that it is so and pick up your pen and journal anyway. Be gentle with yourself, but try to keep moving. It is like exercise. We know it is good for us. We know we will feel physically good, mentally more alert and less depressed and noble to boot. But still we resist and find excuses. I swim every morning. When people ask how I manage to do that so consistently, I always say, "It is never a decision. I just *do* it. If I asked myself 'should I or shouldn't I?' the answer would always be 'NO!'"

In the next chapter we will talk about how to feel safe in doing this work. We've been doing lots of checking in, which I hope helps you have the confidence to go on. But if you haven't been stopped by fear or resistance yet, a time will come when something in you (a part, I'd bet!) will yell "Halt!" Maybe you won't hear it as a yell. Maybe you will experience it as days or weeks where you don't pick up this book or your journal or you lose one or both. We are going to explore what that might be about and how you can deal with it

Chapter 5
SAFETY AND CONTROL

Any time we do personal growth work, it is important to feel safe enough to move into unknown territory. Being safe enough to move forward is a prerequisite to moving! Everyone has a part that has the job of protecting them and keeping control over things. These two tasks usually are performed by the same part. A good general name for it is the Controller/Protector. I think of this part as a gate-keeper. It is the subpersonality that decides what is safe and who needs to come out. It doesn't always have control over what is going on, but it tries. Some people have very busy Controller/Protector parts that get over worked. When those parts get a chance to speak for themselves, they often express being tired. This part wants to keep you safe—from every danger imaginable. It might think some kinds of personal growth work are too dangerous. It might just think climbing mountains, or sky diving is dangerous. But if it thinks something is unsafe for you, it will try to stop you from doing it.

The Controller/Protector is an important part to identify and allow to speak. If this part of you is not recognized and honored, it very well may keep you from working. You may be saying to yourself, "I am too busy" or "I planned to do it yesterday, but the dog threw up" or "I don't get this. I'm probably just too dumb (or smart, or old, or young)" But the Controller/Protector (let's call it CP from now on) is really saying, "This stuff is scary. Who knows what you might find out? I don't like it. Somebody might read your journal and think you are nuts. This is a one-way ticket to the loony farm," or your own personal version of all that.

SESSION FOUR—GIVING THE CONTROLLER/PROTECTOR THE FLOOR

Are you willing to allow yourself to explore the CP part of you? Remember it will probably have a different name than this. Since I have to call it something, I will use CP to talk about it. You can insert your own personal name for this part. I call mine The Old Man and he holds lots of reins in his hands.

Close your eyes and go inside for a moment.

Allow an image of the Controller/Protector part of you to emerge. Can you see it, feel it, hear it? Take a moment to get as full a sense of this part as you can. Remember no editing—what comes is what you need to address. How old is the Controller/Protector? What gender? How is it dressed? Notice the facial expression, posture, demeanor. See if you can allow yourself to become this part. Usually the Controller/Protector is glad to oblige! Controller/Protectors usually like to have air time. They often want to claim they are the self. Experience your

Controller/Protector as fully as you can. Then step back into your self. Can you feel the shift? This is a part of you, not all of who you are.

Now let's try some dialogue with the Controller/Protector part. Begin with the "self" (s):

self (s): *CP are you willing to talk to me?*

Controller/Protector (CP): *Sure*

s: *Tell me about how you operate in my life.*

CP: *[Fill in your own Controller/Protector words here.]*

s: *How do you feel about my exploring my parts?*

CP: *[Fill in your own CP words here].*

Let the CP talk as long as it wants (if you can stand it!) Remember it is crucial to honor every part. This is an important part of you (as it will probably be glad to tell you). It keeps you safe in many ways and keeps things under control. It will be an important ally in learning about the other parts. But it also may sabotage you if it thinks letting a part out is dangerous. You have to be sure you are working at a pace the Controller/Protector feels comfortable with or you may find yourself blocked and not understand why. If that happens, you need to come back to CP and find out what is going on. You do that by dialoguing some more with the CP.

I like to tell Controller/Protector parts that we can make a deal. I promise I won't be devious in trying to get around it and it promises that if it feels uncomfortable it will show up and talk to me directly instead of sabotaging my work. This usually works well. You might want to try making a deal similar to this. You are probably beginning to discover that your parts will let you know what they think about things. They will let you know when my suggestions don't make sense to them. Follow the lead of your parts whenever there is a conflict between my suggestions and theirs.

TAKING STOCK

How are you feeling about what is happening? Do you still feel you are not quite getting it? There are exercises in the appendix that will help. They are there for practice, clarification, and enrichment of the process.

If you are beginning to feel this is fascinating, it is working for you! Since we are all more than a little ego-centric, most people are amazed and delighted when they start to get feedback from their parts. It seems incredible that things come out that were not in our conscious awareness before. This is a good time to state that it was already there. This is a technique for helping to bring this material into conscious awareness.

We are tapping into unconscious material. It is exciting and fun but it can also be somewhat unsettling. It is like dreams that shake us up. It is important to remember that a protective part of you will take care of your well being (likely CP). You can trust yourself and your unconscious. The unsettled feeling comes because there is a reason why some material is not conscious— some things go underground because they are too painful or disturbing and the CP protects us from them. My experience in working with many students and clients using this technique is that the unconscious only releases what we are able to manage.

As you continue this work, if it feels to you that there is more stuff churning within you and you are reluctant to proceed, you may want to consult a therapist. Together you can explore what causes your dis-ease with this process and whether you may be ready to do some therapeutic work. It is my (not unbiased) opinion that we all need therapy at repeated intervals in our lives. It is a matter of self-exploration and personal growth—NOT pathology. If you were not a person who is interested in self-exploration and personal growth, you would not have read past the first paragraph of this book. If the title is pertinent, you would probably not even have taken it off the shelf. People who have an interest in this kind of book are often people who have already had some therapy. If you have not, now or at some future time in your life, you might want to consider it. Journaling and parts work really is a way of doing your own therapy. But if you feel uncomfortable with what is happening, finding someone to coach you and guide you is a good idea. [See the Appendix, page 138 for suggestions on choosing a therapist.]

The unconscious tries to hold onto things. That is why your journal is so important. You will want to keep track of as much of what is happening for you as possible. If you have never recorded your dreams, this may be a good time to start (or to start up again). I have a theory that says the minute my feet touch the floor, the dream flows out my feet and is lost! Keep a pad by your bed in case you have the same flowing out your feet problem that I have! I scribble it down in the dark. Some people use a tape recorder—but then you have to listen to it! And probably write it down. And if you have a partner in your bed, you may get a bit of flack about talking in his or her sleep!

Now that you have had some experience with your own parts and the dialogue, we are going to take a brief break from all this hard work you have been doing. We'll take a look at some behind-the-scenes stuff. I hope you will enjoy learning more about my favorite psychological theory. It is called, psychosynthesis. Isn't that the best psychobabble word you have ever heard? Sounds like we are going to synthesize all the psychos out there! But I think you will like how it helps us understand more what makes us who we are.

Chapter 6
SOME THEORETICAL BACKGROUND

Okay, I admit it, my academic part is creeping into this. I have to follow my own advice—honor the parts and pay attention! So we take a little divergent path and discuss some of the ideas behind these ideas. If you don't want to know, or at least don't want to know *now*, feel free to move on to Chapter 7 where we will resume doing the work. You can always come back to this material later if you decide you might find it interesting.

Roberto Assagioli was the Italian doctor who first talked about subpersonalities. He was working and writing in the early 1900s along with Sigmund Freud and Carl Jung. Freud introduced the idea of the unconscious and separated the personality into the id, ego, and superego. Jung proposed that there are archetypes, or various aspects of the personality that are universal. His idea was that we see these archetypal personality traits in many people and that the archetypes think and act similarly. Assagioli developed a theoretical framework that he called psychosynthesis. It is the foundation of much of my psychotherapeutic work. It incorporates some of Freud's and Jung's ideas and provides an expanded view of the personality.

The major attraction for me to psychosynthesis is that it adds a spiritual dimension to psychology. Assagioli suggests that the unconscious not only includes what Freud theorized, but also a higher unconscious which is our link to the spiritual dimension. Assagioli also uses the word "transpersonal," which simply means "that which is beyond the person." Higher unconscious material can be suppressed just as lower unconscious material can. Both can be outside of our conscious awareness. To understand what makes us "tick" it is helpful to uncover what is suppressed in both the higher and lower unconscious. An egg diagram is used to illustrate Assagioli's idea of the structure of the personality.

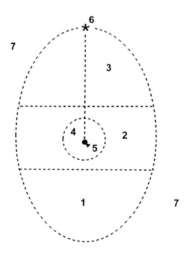

1. **Lower Unconscious:** early repressed material, primitive self or Freud's id. An example: someone who is afraid of water may have no conscious awareness of why but may discover that at age 2 they fell into a pool and nearly drowned. The cause of the fear is unconscious. By making it conscious, we can often find a way to resolve our fear. A strong, pure desire to have what you want when you want it is the primitive self—in most of us it is modified by social training so we can get along with people and thereby meet our need for social connection. The pure desire or primitive self is in the lower unconscious.

2. **Middle Unconscious:** material that is readily available to us. An example is if I ask you what you had for dinner last night or how you feel about your son leaving for college, you can probably pull either up right away. But you were not thinking about it until I asked. This is the part of the diagram that we are working to make bigger. By learning about our parts and how they operate in our lives, we are bringing "stuff" from the lower and higher unconscious into the middle unconscious where we can deal with it, know it, and make decisions about it.

3. **Higher Unconscious:** suppressed material related to spirit and potential of all that we can be. Religious faith would be here but the higher unconscious is not limited to religion. This is the source of our sense that there is something "out there," something beyond our "self." This can also be called the supraconscious.

4. **Conscious:** material that is in the current awareness. It is what you are thinking about in this very moment as in, "What is this lady talking about, is that dog ever going to stop barking,

should I turn off the stove, maybe I really get this, I hope I will have time to call Mom before I leave for class..."

5. **self:** a small "s" is used to differentiate the ego/self from the transpersonal Self. The self is the part of you that is asking the questions in the dialogue, this is "you," around which all the parts are organized.

6. **Self:** the transpersonal part of the personality, the connection to that which is beyond the self. This is the part of us that is in touch with the whole (both of ourselves and the outer world). It does not get emotionally hooked into the events and feelings of our everyday life. Note: There is a distinction between the self with a small "s" and the Self with upper case "S" (i.e. the Transpersonal Self).

7. **Collective Unconscious:** the interconnectedness of life, archetypes, God, Higher Power. The collective unconscious can also be called the universal unconscious. It represents the potential to which we are all connected.

In psychosynthesis, the point of any personal growth work we do is to increase the amount of material we have in our middle unconscious—so that we "know" and can operate from a place of knowing ourselves. The connections we make with the Self and the universal unconscious expand our spiritual life and increase our effectiveness. When we operate from a place of not knowing ourselves or "unconsciously," our lives often feel out of our control. It seems like we are at the mercy of something entirely outside of ourselves. In reality, we are at the mercy of the unclaimed material inside of us. Using the parts language, we are being guided by the part that demands center stage at the moment.

Taking Stock

About now, some of your parts may be screaming, "Enough already!" They are not so interested in the "why" and the "where." They want to speak so you can understand them. They want to get on with the work. But you may have a part that is very excited to know more about the theory. Send that part straight to the appendix where you will find references. Luckily someone else has already written all of this down. We will deal with as much of it as necessary to clarify and make sense of what we are doing. You can take your academic/learner part to the library or book store and allow it to read to its heart's content.

Are you ready to get back to work? Get your journal out and we will learn next about making a map. Chapter 7 leads us through an intuitive process of mapping our parts. If you like to be creative, it will be a good opportunity to play.

Playful Child

Controller
Protector

Scared
One

Critic

ME!

Perfectionist

Vulnerable Child

Chapter 7
YOUR SUBPERSONALITY MAP

Now we have met the Controller/Protector and learned enough
about it to understand what is probably going on when we feel
the work is blocked. I suspect that Controller/Protectors are
somewhat over cautious and tend to think they can handle everything and we don't need to know any more. Make sure your
Controller/Protector knows you appreciate all its efforts on your
behalf and that you sincerely believe you are going to make its
job easier through self-understanding and integration of the
parts.

It always amazes me that as much as I use this technique and
know it works, I can struggle for a long time with a problem or
dis-ease before it occurs to me to practice what I preach and
begin a dialogue in my journal. Often I think that is my

Controller/Protector who thinks it can keep everything under control and we don't have to go off on a dangerous search- and-find mission. Remember, my Controller/Protector is called The Old Man and he holds a bunch of reins in his hands. He has been known to sit down on a couch and tuck the reins under a couch leg. He is a good guy, really and often very wise. But he'd just as soon sit on something as begin working on it. Guess he thinks there is always more danger in exploring than staying put!

SESSION FIVE—MAKING YOUR SUBPERSONALITY MAP

It is time to make a map of all the parts you have discovered so far. Don't worry if you have only Part 1 and Part 2 and the Controller/Protector. We will get a more complete map very soon. The map is a depiction of the parts and all the information you have about them.

A helpful way to diagram your parts is to make a drawing like this:

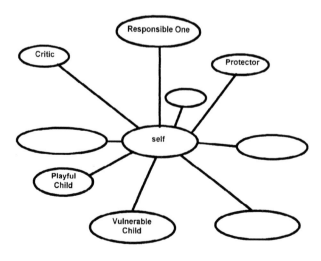

The "self" in the center of the diagram is the same "self" that it is the middle of the egg diagram we looked at earlier. The parts are arranged in relationship to the "self." Make sure you always have at least one more oval than parts you already know. This implies that there are always parts we haven't identified yet. It is important to understand that we never know everything (or everyone, in this case). We want to keep this work open and fluid. If you like to draw, feel free to draw the parts on your map—there is nothing magic about the ovals, improvise if you like. Hopefully you will end up with a paper that shows you the parts you have so far identified; and that perhaps gives you some insight into how they are in juxtaposition to each other.

Notice how the parts are arranged in the diagram. Take notes if there is something that particularly strikes you. For example, do you suspect there is some significance to what parts are next to each other? Opposite from one another? At the top of the diagram? At the bottom? Sort of outside and left out?

List next to each subpersonality the qualities you know this part has. For example, the Critic: judgmental, punitive, observant, relentless. You almost surely do not know everything about this part yet. But listing the qualities you do know fleshes out your map.

Try not to over analyze or be too intellectual about all of this. Remember this is an intuitive process. There is no "right" way to do it and there certainly is no "wrong" way. We want to take notice of things—not pin them down. When you find yourself losing sight of this, ask "who?" (what part of me?) and "What do I know about the part of me that keeps trying to get it right? or that analyzes it to death?" Using questions like these, as you go along, will help you identify new parts and/or flesh out ones you already know.

If there are new parts that occur to you as you make your map, this is a good time to flesh them out in your journal. Do this the same way we have learned about parts previously. You might want to get out your art materials again and work with images, color, and form. Your map might be more than words. Feel free to elaborate it in any way that you would like.

Melissa has given me permission to share her map with you. She made this map when she first began to work with the idea of sub-personalities. Since then, it has changed considerably. For example, the storm door (which kept out both good and bad) has become a screen door. Now it can screen what is to come in or go out. Melissa can make more choices about what she wants to let into her inner world and what she wants to let out of it. Don't consider your map a completed project but a work in progress. As you continue to work in your journal, you will identify new parts. You can add them to your map.

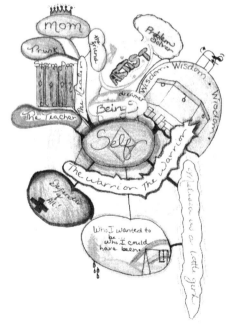

TAKING STOCK

Is it time to remind you to be gentle with yourself? You may be having a ball with all of this. Or you may be struggling every inch of the way. Make space for either of these positions and all the spaces in-between. Chances are you won't be at either end of that continuum for too long. The best way to get past blocks is to give yourself permission to be where you are until you are ready to be somewhere else. I find when I am being too critical about how I am doing something like this, or about where I am, that it helps me to write in my journal: Be gentle with yourself. It is okay to be where you are. Who is having a hard time? Who needs some reassurance?

We are now ready to learn about using the dialogue technique to resolve conflicts in our lives. We will start easy. We will also continue to address resistance. Resistance is a persistent partner in our inner workings and self exploration. It shows up at the most critical moments. So we will take a closer look at this essential element of personal work and try to learn how to deal with it.

Chapter 8
THE HORNS OF A DILEMMA

When we talked at the beginning about why we would want to
see ourselves in parts, one of the answers was to resolve conflicts
or make decisions. This is a very useful part of the work and one
that I often have to remind myself to do. It is interesting that we
often stay stuck even when we have tools to help us. I think it is
about that old adage, "better the trouble we know than the trouble
we do not know." In the next session, we'll try to move past our
own resistance.

SESSION SIX—USING DIALOGUE TO RESOLVE CONFLICT

For the sake of practice, let's return to the idea of using dialogue
to resolve a conflict in your life. Choose an issue that has trou-
bled you lately. It can be as mundane as whether to paint that

room blue or terra cotta (remember my example at the beginning of this text?) It can be something complex and deeply troubling like whether to stay in a relationship. You are getting more accustomed to this process but may not feel ready to tackle something really serious. Let your intuition guide you and trust you are ready to do whatever comes to mind.

Begin by stating the dilemma in your journal. Then using s, or your initial, to represent the ego/self ask the question, "Who needs to talk about this issue?" Allow the pen to move across the page. Remind yourself you can trust whatever comes.

If you seem to be having difficulty getting a response to flow forth, you might want to check with our new friend, the Controller/Protector. Remember that the CP is looking out for your best interests—take any input from this part seriously. With some gentle discussion of the CP's hesitance, you may get permission to proceed. If there is still resistance, ask what would make it safe enough to go on. Sometimes limiting the scope of what you are trying to do will make the difference. For example, try agreeing that all you will do in this first attempt is to hear what each part has to say and learn what the issues are. Then you'll check back in with the CP to see if it feels safe to begin working toward resolution.

If the CP says it is okay to go on but you still feel scattered and more than one part wants to talk at a time, take a moment to center. This term "center" refers to pulling in our awareness so that we feel present within ourselves. (Check Appendix, page 132 for an exercise to help you do this if it is not apparent to you how to settle down and be centered in your "self.") From your centered self, acknowledge that you are making a choice to do this work and to allow what needs to come. By doing this we are engaging our will, recognizing that the control comes from within and that it is a decision to do the work.

Now go back to your dialogue. Have the self (s) say, "Okay, guys, everyone will get a chance to express an opinion. But you have to talk one at a time for me to understand what is happening. Tell me if you want to talk and we'll be sure everyone gets a chance." Now you know you are in for a time commitment. Make sure you have enough time or that you promise to come back (and be sure you *do*).

Talk to the parts, with "s" as the questioning side of the conversation. It is confusing if the parts talk to each other and is better to always have them go through "s." The primary goal is to increase your conscious awareness of how your subpersonalities feel about this issue and what each needs. Be sure to ask about their needs and wants. This is the essential issue for them. Ask them what they do for you in your life, if they think they get enough air time, what they would do if they had more/less.

You may be surprised at how much awareness can change things. It is also okay to negotiate with the parts once you understand them. You may be surprised at how cooperative they can be. It seems to make a big difference to subpersonalities when they feel heard and honored. They usually have more trust in you to make good decisions and to take care of them than you would think. They will often back off of a hard-held position or be willing to concede something in exchange for an assurance of something else. Do you remember the principle: Every part has a positive intent? All of the subpersonalities truly want what is best for the whole. However, sometimes a part has a distorted idea of what is best. Be conscious of looking for the positive intent. Express your gratitude when you uncover it. Be gentle with your parts.

If a part is determined to hold fast to a position and it feels to you this part needs to change before you can make a good decision, try this question. "If you allowed [insert in the brackets whatever you think needs to happen] what do you think would happen?" No matter what the answer is, ask "And if [...] happened?" Keep asking that question, using the answers that come for the next question until you feel you have reached the core. Often this brings you to a place of recognition of a fear about the change that is needed. Once a fear is identified, we are often able to say, "Yes that is possible but it probably won't happen. It is probably worth taking this risk to get what I want." If that is not the case, now you know why you are stuck here and may need to step back and reconsider where you want to go.

An example: *If I allowed [myself to do this parts work] then maybe I would learn more about myself. And if [I learned more about myself] maybe I wouldn't like what I found out. And if [I didn't like what I found out] I would know I am a bad person. And if I knew I was a bad person I couldn't stand it. And if I couldn't stand it maybe I would go crazy.*

This is a pretty catastrophic fear! I just let it roll and that is what came! But can you see how you may get yourself to your core fear about moving forward with a decision about anything? If the above were your piece, you'd want to ask, "Do I really believe I would go crazy? Do I really believe I am a bad person? Am I willing to take the risk that I can find out about myself, know some things I do not like, and still hold onto both my sanity and my sense of being an okay person?" If the answers run to "Yes, I think I would go crazy and no, I don't think I am an okay person and I don't want to know!" then hopefully you would recognize how smart you are to be resisting this work. Your

Controller/Protector would be firmly in charge and setting appropriate limits. You would be able to decide to stop or to get some help from a therapist to work through your fear.

TAKING STOCK

Are you beginning to wonder if my mother was right? Does it feel a little crazy to be talking to yourself and answering? What did you learn by doing the last dialogue? Did it bring you any closer to resolving the dilemma? Are you still stuck but feeling more knowledgeable about what keeps you stuck? I hope by now you are beginning to feel that this is working and if it is working, then it is not crazy!

Are you getting to know the Controller/Protector part better? The Critic? This is valuable information so don't get discouraged. We have a tendency to think certain parts are out to get us. But if they are talking to you, I bet by now you are beginning to learn that they aren't so bad. They really do have your best interest at heart. And they really are workable.

It is possible that you did not get to work on the dilemma you chose but instead were side-tracked into dealing with hesitant or resistant parts. That is still valuable learning. Try another session later that addresses the dilemma again. Don't give up! You are doing fine. Whatever is coming is exactly what is supposed to be there.

Now we'll explore some samples of dialogue work. The next chapter gives you a chance to see how someone else's work looks.

Chapter 9
SAMPLE DIALOGUES

I have deliberately refrained from giving you extended examples of dialogue. I wanted you to get a chance to see what emerges for you. Whatever you have written is absolutely right for you.

In this chapter, though, I am going to give you some examples. It might help you with what kinds of questions to ask. Warning: Don't let your Critic or Judge compare my dialogue samples to yours and then diminish yours. Maybe they won't be very similar. If you learned something about your subpersonalities, then your work was helpful to you. If it felt like fun, it was worth doing. If my examples help you deepen what you are doing, that is good. If there are dissimilarities to yours, trust that yours are right for *you*. In this work it is essential to trust your own intuitive sense of what is right. If something in you is saying, "This work is not right for me," allow yourself to stop right now. There is no one right way to do self-exploration and personal growth. You can always pass this book on to a friend who may love it!

DIALOGUE ONE

Let's begin with the "paint the room" dilemma.

Purpose: To resolve the issue, "Shall I paint my study blue or terra cotta?"

self (s): *Who needs to speak to this issue?*

Chorus: *We do!*

s: *I need you to speak one at a time. I promise to hear each of you. Who will go first?*

Contented One (CO): *Me! I love blue. My favorite times are when we go the beach or the woods and we can sit quietly and look at the sky and the water. It makes all of us feel calm and placid. It is soothing.*

s: *Quiet and calm are important to you, CO.*

CO: *Yes. I think it is good for everyone when we can do that. I want the study to be blue so when you feel agitated you can sit in the study and feel soothed.*

Artist (A): *Can I speak now?*

s: *CO are you ready to let Artist have the floor?*

CO: *Sure.*

A: *I am the artist part of you. I think blue is mundane and a drag. Remember when we were in Arizona and saw all the beautiful colored stone?*

s: *Yes. I loved that.*

A: *Well, I want the room terra cotta because it reminds me of that. It is warm and more exciting and will help you stir up the creative juices.*

s: *It sounds like you want inspiration to create?*

A: *Yeah. That is it. If the room feels more vibrant, I will come out more often.*

s: *That makes a lot of sense. I want to create in this room. But I also want to use the room for serenity. My life gets hectic and I need a quiet place.*

Does anyone else have an opinion?

Critic (C): *You bet! You are such a pain. Why do you let all this drivel go on? Can't you make even a simple decision like this without all this hoopla? Blue, schmoo. Pick something that works and get on with it.*

s: *It is hard for you, Critic, when I dilly-dally over a decision. You want precise, quick action and for it always to be right.*

C: *You've got it!*

s: *Well, guys I am thinking here of a compromise. I don't want to delay any longer. But when you, Critic, start criticizing me, I feel stymied. I can't move because I feel like I am going to do it wrong. We are down to two colors and I am going to try to negotiate a compromise. Will you back off and let this move forward?*

C: *I guess. Just do it right.*

s: *Well, it feels like there isn't an absolute right here and that both colors are very appealing. Given how hectic my life can be, I think I need the walls to be blue to provide serenity. I'll hang a* *picture of water in a forest to expand that theme. But I will be sure to decorate with my Arizona artifacts—those pretty terra cotta vases and the masks I bought there. Then I can have the serenity you want CO and the inspiration that will keep the creativity of Artist alive.*

A: *Now we are talking!*

CO: *I can live with that!*

DISCUSSION

Can you see how opposing parts can and will compromise their positions? There is wisdom in the self to negotiate and create a solution. But we often are stuck because we can't sort out the needs and wants of the parts without addressing them directly. When they have been heard, the parts are usually willing to back off. Remember you are conducting this orchestra and make the final decisions.

The Critic was a part of being stuck, but before the dialogue there was not conscious awareness of this. It is not obvious from the statement of the dilemma that any parts except the two who have an investment in a certain color, are involved. But in the dialogue, the Critic emerges. When we are hearing that critical/judgmental voice in our ear, it is hard to make compromises or to resolve any issue. We get stuck in the "You have to get it right" mire and become immobilized. It is scary to move when we fear retribution for making an error.

In this dialogue, the self acknowledges the Critic's position, showing empathy by understanding what is important to it. However, the self does not give in to the Critic's demands for perfection. It is my experience that when parts are acknowledged and heard, they will be easily satisfied even when their needs cannot be directly met. The self cannot provide a perfect solution. But the compromise is enough to satisfy the Critic. And it acknowledges what is important to both the Artist and the Contented One.

DIALOGUE TWO

In an effort to operate from a new paradigm, I dialogue sometimes rather than confront issues directly with a person in my life. In the new paradigm, we can choose how we are going to feel about something. So anger becomes an option instead of a foregone conclusion. I find the dialogue helps me decide what I am going to feel and "who" is going to deal with the situation.

Purpose: To understand why a part of me wants to be angry with my husband over what is really a small issue.

self (s): *A part of me wants to be really angry. How dare he!?*

Fury(F): *Yeah!*

s: *Oh Fury, it isn't worth it!*

F: *Why?*

s: *Because. Life is too short. I love him. He reacts this way because he is feeling abandoned and disconnected.*

F: *Ach. Why should I care?*

s: *You don't have to but I want to. This is our life—this man. We have way too little left of it, no matter how long it lasts, to waste even a minute being angry and distant.*

Maskless Me (the wise part, MM): *Well said!!*

s: *Thanks MM. I'm glad to have you in this conversation.*

MM: *Don't let anger eat at your belly.*

s: *No. And it was a wonderful day, sublime in many ways. I enjoyed being with him. Also we didn't find time for making love this weekend.*

MM: *That could give you a short fuse!*

F: *Yeah!*

s: *Yes. But it was a matter of time, energy and priorities. We had a lovely, super day, then this small incident. Let it go!*

MM: *Yes. Really!*

F: *Oh, shucks!*

s: *What do you need, Fury?*

F: *Nada. I just want to knock his block off.*

s: *Yeah, yeah, yeah.*

F: *Okay. So I don't get to. You could tell him.*

s: *Only that I love him. I'm going to let him work his mad off in his own way.*

F: *Wimp!*

s: *Okay. Sticks and stones...*

F: *Phooey!*

s: *Even still.*

F: *Whatever.*

DISCUSSION

Obviously, there is not a resolution to this dialogue. I believe what helps is that the Fury gets an opportunity to voice its stance. There is a tendency here for the s to be somewhat flip with this part. Another dialogue might get even better results with clearer support for the agenda of the Fury. However, the result in this real life example is that I was able to choose to be loving and friendly and let go of my end of the dissonance between my husband and me. When I come from a place of true center, I find that arguments don't happen and his "mad" doesn't last any longer than mine!

Can you see how parts just show up in both of these dialogues? That never ceases to amaze me, even after years of experience. I am still intrigued and delighted with the changes that seem to emerge from merely allowing the unconscious to bring forth whatever it chooses.

TAKING STOCK

Even though you haven't done any more work, let's talk a little about how you are doing now that you have read some samples.

These dialogues are short compared to many in my own journal. Length is not the measuring criteria, though. You may find you are brief and succinct and get good results. You may be wordy and still get good results. If it is working, don't try to fix it. Certainly, don't try to make it more like mine. The first of these dialogues is just made up! (When my decorating-savvy daughter read it she was very unsatisfied by the conclusion. But I hope it makes some points anyway.) The second is copied directly from one of my journal entries (with only a little editing—because I am sharing publicly, I get to edit!).

Are you feeling frustrated that your work is not flowing easily? It can be difficult to learn to let go and allow the work to flow. It is still early in the learning process. Try not to be discouraged. If you are feeling blocked, try asking the question, "Who is having trouble with this process?" Dialogue with the part that answers. If you do not get an answer, try addressing the Critic or the Controller/Protector. Try each of them.

Next, we will expand our understanding of the parts you have identified. And I will throw in some more theory. I think you will find it both interesting and, I hope, fun. The theory gives you a chance to rest from all this hard personal work you are doing. And when your friends tell you they don't get it, you'll be able to explain a little more about where it all comes from!

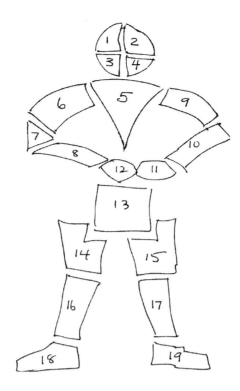

Chapter 10
FLESHING OUT THE PARTS

We are going to take time to do some exercises that will help you make your parts more clearly defined. This is an ongoing process. Recently, I learned a technique called the "Art Journal" and applied it to acknowledging my subpersonalities. In doing that work, I feel I learned some more about each of them and how they "look" in my life. (See Appendix, page 136 "The Art Journal" for a *how-to* exercise.)

SESSION SEVEN—BECOMING THE PARTS

Look back at the map you made of your subpersonalities—the one with the ovals and their names. Choose two parts that seem to you opposites or at least very different. You will need some space to do this—at least a four foot diameter circle in which you can stand. You will probably also want privacy!

Stand in the middle of your circle. Take a deep breath and allow yourself to center. Feel your "self" in the middle of this circle.

Now (I prefer closed eyes but that is up to you) step to the left of center, standing on the circumference of your circle. Step "into" one of the parts you have chosen. Allow yourself to become that part. Be aware of how you are dressed, how you stand, the expression on your face, how you feel. Let yourself become the part as much as possible. Then step back into the center. Take a deep breath and separate your "self" from this part. Feel yourself centered again. Now step to the right. Allow yourself to become the other part. Be aware of how you are dressed, how you stand, the expression on your face, how you feel. Experience this part as much as possible. Now step back into the center. Take a deep breath again and separate your "self" from this part. Feel yourself centered again.

Take notes in your journal about this experience. How did you feel doing it? What are you aware of about each part now?

Set up a dialogue with one of the parts. Go back to basics and ask the part what its role is in your life, all those questions we asked in Chapter 2, Session One, page 10. It is often helpful to end the dialogue by asking, "Is there anything else you want me to know?" Now, of course, dialogue with the other part.

After each dialogue take some notes. What is new in terms of awareness? Are there any surprises? Did any other parts butt in? Did you let them? If you did not, make a commitment to let that part speak later. Are you beginning to hear recurring themes? Did moving into the part help you get a clearer definition of it? Did the dialogue seem deeper? How are you feeling?

Watch out for the Critic! Remember what you wrote is what was supposed to be written right now. Even if you did not feel there was any major decision made, or earth-shattering revelations, I suspect you will find that this piece of work makes a difference for you.

Please do not skimp on the note-taking part at the end of your dialogues. This is important, especially if you are not working in a group or with a therapist where you will talk about your dialogues. It is called "grounding" and is how we bring the work into our real lives. This stuff can get sort of unreal or illusory if it is not grounded. The grounding helps keep you from feeling scattered. It brings you back together.

MORE ABOUT THE PROCESS—REASSURANCE

When I do presentations about this process, someone usually asks me, "Isn't this sort of like multiple personalities or schizophrenia?" Even clients sometimes say, "Am I going to be like Sybil?" (a multiple personality). The "split" in schizophrenia is an entirely different thing. I don't think we need to get into a definition of that right here but it is not a risk in doing this work. Schizophrenia is a mental illness with a chemical/biological component. We can't create it by doing work like this.

I used to answer the above queries about multiple personality and Sybil with a firm, "No, it is nothing like that." But as my therapeutic work matured and I found myself treating some clients with this dissociative disorder, I realized that it is far more connected than I thought. The difference is that in the multiple personality, the boundaries between parts are very rigid. It is possible for the ego/self not to be aware of certain parts and for the parts to behave without the knowledge of the ego/self. Many psychiatrists believe this condition is extremely rare. Some therapists have seen numerous clients who appear to dissociate in this way. It is a condition that develops because of some major trauma, like sexual abuse, from early childhood. I now see a continuum instead of an absolute division. The work is very similar and the goals the same: awareness and integration. The difference is in the conscious awareness of the ego/self and of the parts.

You do not need to be afraid that you could become a multiple personality by doing this work. If you have had (or think you may have had) dissociative periods in your life (times when you seem to "lose yourself"), this work may not be good for you to do without a therapist. My guess is people with this concern have not read this far! But if you are worried, consult a professional (See Choosing A Therapist, Appendix page 138).

I have also been asked (as recently as two days ago!) if this is not contrary to what therapy is supposed to do. Doesn't therapy try to help us hold it together? Isn't separating ourselves out into parts counter to that goal? The answer is that it is quite the contrary. When we recognize the parts of ourselves, we are creating self-awareness. Through self-awareness, we have informed choice in how we are going to feel and behave. This is a metaphor. It is similar to how children use the play in play therapy to resolve issues. Many play therapists believe it is not necessary to ever talk directly with the child about what the play means. The work is the play and the play is the work! I see this parts work in that way. That is why the dialogue works even when there is no obvious resolution. You don't have to analyze the metaphor to get the benefits.

When you can let go and trust yourself, this work is like play. You will find it fun much of the time. Children may not always be having fun when they play. But they are doing what they need to do to learn life's tasks and resolve their internal conflicts. (I am talking here about creative/pretend play, not Nintendo!) So even if it is not fun or doesn't feel like "work," often it is working. I think if you are still with me, you know this at some level.

SOME THEORY AGAIN

In psychosynthesis, Assagioli (remember this guy, he's the Italian psychiatrist who developed psychosynthesis and suggested the idea of subpersonalities) works from some basic assumptions. It might be helpful for you to know what these are since much of this work is based on Assagioli's ideas.

1. Each individual is unique. That's why I so often remind you to trust your own sense of what is right for you. There is no theory or technique that fits everyone.

2. Answers are already within each person. This work is from within. We are always looking for the part that knows the answer and can help us resolve the internal conflict. We need to trust ourselves that we know what is right for us and start where we are not where we think we should be.

3. There is meaning—in the world, in the universe, within the person. Unless we experience some connection to the greater whole, we feel that something is missing.

4. All persons have potential to live their transpersonal or higher selves. This means we go a step beyond merely integrating the personality. The step beyond is synthesis and is an ideal. We are never fully "there" but always moving toward synthesis.

5. All persons have everything needed within them to grow toward integration and synthesis. Personal growth is an inner-directed process. We get help from outside (books, therapists, friends, gurus) but only through looking inward can we truly move.

6. People can grow and change. This is an important assumption. Sometimes we feel so stuck we think maybe there is no hope for us. We see others who seem unable to change. Change is a choice that even the most entrenched can make.

7. **Everyone has blocks.** Self exploration can help us identify the blocks and go beyond them. Blocks make us feel hopeless and stuck. But there is a way to get past the blocks.

8. **For each person there is a center which is an integrating center of consciousness.** We feel this center in those moments when we are at peace with ourselves. We can reach this center through conscious work.

9. **The ultimate purpose is to express more fully the transpersonal Self in the world.** Self-understanding brings us into closer contact with the transpersonal Self and through its expression, with the spiritual.

TAKING STOCK

Well, have I given you more theory stuff than you want to know? I hope you are remembering you can skip anything that bores you. Some people just want to do the work and forget all the whys and wherefores. Feel free. I am thinking that others may want to understand a little more about what is behind it.

Anytime you run into any part of this book that disturbs you or stops you dead in your tracks, the question you need to ask is, "Who is bothered by this?" If you keep asking "Who?" you will begin to uncover hidden fears and areas of dis-ease. Usually these will dissipate when you have identified the part and heard its concerns. If not, you probably need to pay attention and stop! That is a good time to consult with a therapist about your concerns and fears.

We are now going to look a little at the structure of what we are doing here. Hopefully, it will make the process flow better. We'll also deal with how to ground your work so it doesn't get to feeling "all talk and no action" or too ethereal.

Chapter 11
EXTENDING THE PROCESS

We are involved in a process that has some structure. You have already been following the structure diagrammed below. First, you have been writing in your journal the dilemma or issue to be addressed. That is the Statement of the Problem. Then, you are asking, "Who needs to talk about this?" That is the Identification of Parts Involved. Next you are allowing the parts to talk, the Dialogue. Then you are writing about the experience, looking at what you have learned and asking how this applies to your real life. That is called Grounding.

Statement of the Problem

Identification of Parts Involved

Dialogue

↓

Grounding

EXPANDING THE GROUNDING

The grounding piece can be expanded by: talking it out with a friend who really gets this or a therapist who knows this work; art journal work; or a "call to action." The latter is when we now know what we need to *do* and we make a commitment to ourselves to act. Not every dialogue requires a call to action. The ways to expand the grounding are described below.

Talking it out: While not always available, talking it out is probably the first choice. If you and a friend are trying to work this book together, you should plan to meet on a regular basis to provide an opportunity to ground your individual work with each other. Reading your dialogue is one option but do not allow that practice to get you into writing to an "audience." That can be deadly to your work. It is sometimes best to read sections, rather than whole pieces. Tell your friend the insights you have gleaned from the piece of work you are discussing. Talk about how you see the insights being integrated into your life. Ask for feedback if you want it (feedback should only be given by request or permission). Your friend may have some other suggestions about what a particular dialogue could mean. An interesting way to share ideas about another person's work is to say, "If this were my dialogue, I would be wondering about...." This method is less likely to offend or feel like criticism or judgment. It also may provide insight into the speaker's own process.

Art Journal: Choose images or words and create a collage that feels representative to you of the work you have done in the writing. Perhaps you will make several pages in your journal, combining whatever choice of techniques you like. The pages will help you have a firmer sense of the work that has taken place and may add more insights. You may want to draw or make a collage to represent how your life will be different with the insight gained. See the Art Journal section in the Appendix page 136.

Call to Action: This is a commitment to yourself to act as a result of the dialogue. Not every dialogue requires a call to action. Be careful that your Critic or Perfectionist doesn't push you to make commitments you do not feel ready to make. However, if an action seems appropriate, you may find it helpful to write a statement that is either your "call to action" or a brief summary of what you have gleaned from this piece of work. An example from our sample dialogue on the room color choice would be: "I will buy the paint tomorrow and begin painting the room this weekend." If the "call to action" is more difficult to execute because you have been avoiding it, try writing your "call to action" statement on a large piece of paper and posting it where you will see it several times a day. Call a friend to share your "call to action."

TAKING STOCK

The above activities help to make this dialogue work relate to your real life. We are not only having fun, we want the work to move us along in our self-awareness and perhaps in our behavior in the world.

Are you beginning to see changes in your life, your attitudes, and your relationships? That is the real reward for all of this work. If it is not happening yet, pay more attention to this grounding idea. It is an important part of the process that we sometimes want to overlook. If we are in a hurry to get on to the next piece, we might skip right over the application part. Then we fail to ground what we are doing in our real life and the work becomes a meaningless exercise.

Can you see that it is helpful to have someone to work with? I believe as social beings, we need to share our growth experiences and get feedback from someone who can be objective and has our best interest at heart. It can be fun to work this book with a friend. I lead groups where we do the work together and spend lots of time processing each person's work. What we learn is that we are all connected and that another person's work is also our own. We share by saying, "If this were my work, I'd [know, think, wonder]..."

Sit back, take a few deep breaths, get comfy. We're going to look at theory again. I sure reneged on my initial commitment to leave the theory out. If it doesn't fit for you, don't put it on! Yet this next part is pretty crucial to moving forward from here so I rather hope you'll put your feet up and read Chapter 12.

Chapter 12
STAGES, THE OBSERVER, AND THE WILL

We are back to Assagioli and some of his basic ideas. The three things described in this chapter are important concepts. The idea of the observing part of you will help you assess what is going on for you and get in touch with yourself at a deeper level. The concept of The Will is one of Assagioli's core ideas about how our personality works. It will help you "own" your own stuff and accept both your impetus to move and your resistance. You have already been working through the stages of subpersonality work that I am now going to describe. Again, sometimes it helps to know some of the theory behind what you are doing.

STAGES IN SUBPERSONALITY WORK

1. **Recognition:** Often there is a "recognition reflex" when a person identifies a part. I am always amazed at how often this reflex is there with people who have never heard of parts work nor looked at their inner world in this way. It is an "oh, yes I know this part of me" awareness.

2. **Acceptance:** When we are describing a part, we are accepting it. When we are judging a part, we are not accepting it. It is essential that each part be honored by our acceptance. Sometimes we become aware of a subpersonality that we dislike and do not want to have as part of us. People will say, "I have always hated that part of me. I want to get rid of it." If we reject any part of ourselves, we create a block and can't move on until we disassemble that block. We cannot kill off parts. When threatened with annihilation, they just go underground. They continue to try to get their needs met by behaviors that may be destructive.

3. **Coordination:** This is a refining stage in which we are helping the subpersonality acquire flesh and blood. The part goes from a skeleton to a person. It is in this stage that the idea of sub-'personality' makes more sense because we can see a part as having a form, a look, an age, needs and wants that set it apart and make it feel like an entity in and of itself. The use of the term "energy" for a part makes more sense because we can feel the energy of the part.

4. **Integration:** In the fourth stage, the part (or aspect of the self) begins to cooperate harmoniously with the whole. This is when your orchestra begins to make music! Integration becomes apparent as we do the dialogue and find the subpersonalities surprisingly willing to go along with the needs of

the whole. They are willing to change their behavior to make things happen. If you have done the first three stages successfully, this one follows naturally.

5. **Synthesis:** This is the final stage where everything comes together. In reality it is an ideal. There are times when we feel synthesis, when all the parts are working together and we feel absolutely whole and centered. But it is unrealistic to think we could live in that place all of the time. Synthesis also means connected to the transpersonal and in harmony with the universe. While, hopefully, we will feel ourselves more and more in tune, we know we can never live fully in harmony one hundred percent of the time. We are always moving on the path toward synthesis.

CENTER AND THE OBSERVER

Several times as we have worked, I have talked about "centering." If you needed to go to the appendix for a centering exercise or if you were already aware of this concept, perhaps you don't feel it needs explaining. However, it is very central to psychosynthesis work and relevant to our dialogue.

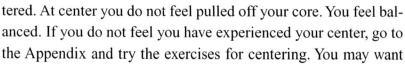

Remember the egg diagram on page 36? At the center is the "I" or "self." When you are feeling fully in that place, you are centered. At center you do not feel pulled off your core. You feel balanced. If you do not feel you have experienced your center, go to the Appendix and try the exercises for centering. You may want to read them into a tape recorder and then play them for yourself so you can truly get into the experience. Some people use meditation or yoga to find their center. There are other ways to get there but it is important to do so. A therapist would know how to help you do this if it feels totally elusive to you.

I am bringing this discussion into focus at this time because as you work with the dialogue on your own, you need to know how to center yourself. If you try to work with one of the renegade parts that wants to be all of you or that seems to be unwilling to work with the rest, you need to know how to bring yourself back to your center. Whenever you feel yourself unbalanced, take time out to center. Use an exercise from the appendix or a method you already have found effective. It is important not to allow negative energies to take over. You always have access to your center. Don't be bullied by a part!

SESSION EIGHT—CALLING ON THE OBSERVER

The Observer part of you is the part that can step outside the "self" and simply observe what is going on. Calling on the Observer when you feel unbalanced is another way to disidentify from the energy of the part with which you are working and by which you may feel unbalanced. Return to center. Ask the Observer to give you an account of what has been happening in your work.

If the concept of the Observer seems vague, try this: Close your eyes. Imagine an objective, observing self stepping outside of your body. Become that observing part. Stand (as the Observer) in front of your body and be aware of what you see. Observe from behind, from above, from each side. Now draw or write your observations. You can do the same exercise with your emotions and with your mind. This observing activates the Observer. The Observer is the one who is observing. It may sound like doublespeak but if you were successful at doing the exercise, take it on faith. If you were not able to do it, try other senses. Imagine an observing part of you touching you for example, exploring your skin texture, temperature, the curves of your body and the texture of your hair. Or try smelling or hearing. Usually one modality will give you access. The part who smells, hears, feels, or sees is the Observer. Are you willing to know the observing part of you?

THE WILL

The use of the question "are you willing?" in the last paragraph brings us to another essential concept in Assagioli's psychosynthesis theory. It is the idea of The Will. Assagioli says we can make choices. He is not talking about will power (like will I eat that chocolate cake or the tangerine for dessert?!) He is talking about the belief that we have within us the ability to choose. Even not choosing is a choice. It pretty much smacks us up the side of the head when we really consider the idea of The Will. It rather makes us responsible, doesn't it? When someone says, "I don't know" to a question about their internal process, I ask if they are *willing* to know. It may not evoke the answer right away but it certainly puts the responsibility for knowing or not knowing squarely where it belongs!

Now before you decide to let the Critic have a field day here, let's get back to the idea of being gentle with ourselves. Sometimes it is a wise choice not to know. Sometimes we are not ready for an answer. The important thing to understand is that we *own* our choice. We acknowledge to ourselves that we can choose to know but have a good reason not to. (Or even not such a good reason!).

Are you getting this idea of The Will? It says, I am responsible for my feelings, my thoughts, and my actions. I have access to my inner world. It is all right to protect myself until I feel safe enough to take the next step. But it is important to acknowledge to myself that I am choosing to stay put—it is not some outside force that withholds the knowledge from me. When I am ready, I can choose to know.

TAKING STOCK

Are you beginning to feel pretty knowledgeable about this parts stuff? I hope so. We have covered a lot of ground in a short space. Probably you are beginning to have some pretty astonishing revelations. I would expect that you have discovered some parts you didn't know were there. Or perhaps you have been told things by your parts that really surprised you. All of this is to be expected. It has probably taken you awhile to get here because you are stopping to do the work along the way.

What, you aren't stopping to do the work as you read along? If you are one of those people who need to get the whole picture before you commit to something, keep reading. But if you are dragging your feet, you need to go back to START! Do remember that if this doesn't feel right to you, it very likely isn't. But if you have read this far and haven't picked up a journal and pen yet, I'm a little suspicious. I am wondering what would keep you reading and "who" is keeping you from writing? Most people for whom this work is inappropriate would have fallen by the wayside long ago. So if you are still here, not writing, and wanting to be then try one or all of these questions:

- **Who likes this enough to keep reading?**
- **Who is the skeptic or who says it won't work?**
- **Who says, "Don't try it?"**

One way to approach our own resistance to something is to ask, "If I allowed myself to do this then...?" Finish the sentence and then ask "And if that, then...?" If this sounds familiar, it is. We did it back when we were dialoguing and trying to discover why a part might be refusing to budge. But if you aren't writing, you probably didn't do the exercise. We are sort of getting to the point of now or never. Are you *willing* to know what is keeping you from trying this?

We have a chapter with fewer paragraphs coming up. But it is not less important for being short! You may look at its title and think you don't need it. "I feel safe enough. I'm doing great." Okay. I'll take your word for it. Take mine! You need this chapter. If not now, later. So dig in.

Chapter 13
A SAFE PLACE

As you continue to dialogue, you will find that you are working on more significant material. As we talk about The Will, this is probably a good time to also talk some more about safety and being gentle with ourselves.

If you are feeling shame, embarrassment, inadequacy, it is probably your Critic at work. If you are feeling frightened, there is probably a vulnerable part (perhaps a child, but not necessarily so) that has been scared to know too much. Maybe there are some scary memories that could come to the surface through the dialogue. Maybe this part is always scared to move, afraid of taking a wrong turn, of failing, of doing it wrong. Before you work on this, you may want to take time to create a safe place to which you can retreat if things get too frightening.

SESSION NINE—CREATING A SAFE PLACE

If something in you is saying, "yes, yes" then try this imagery exercise. (Even if you aren't reacting much to this talk about fear, you might enjoy this and it is always good to have a safe place— I use mine when I go to the dentist!) You may want to audio tape the exercise and then follow it as you listen with your eyes closed. Or if you are working with a friend, you could read it for one another. It is hard to do imagery work while you are reading the directions. However, it can be done— by reading through the exercise first, then taking it one step at a time.

Exercise: Begin by using whatever works best for you to center yourself. Make sure you are in a comfortable place where you can be assured of privacy and quiet. From center, allow an image to emerge of a place that you enjoy and that feels safe to you. It could be a beach, a woods, your backyard, your bed. The important thing is that it feels safe. Be aware that in imagery you can have whatever you need. If this place would be safe if only you had a baseball bat, it is yours! If what you need is a hand to hold, try to allow your own wise or nurturing part to be present. Or allow a person who represents safety be with you. Place yourself in this scene. Be aware of what you see. Notice what you feel— like temperature, breezes, textures. What do you smell? What are the sounds you hear? The use of your senses will help put you more thoroughly in your scene. Make it as detailed as you would like. Spend some time here. Absorb the feeling of safety. As you prepare to leave, be aware that you can return here any time you wish. You may want to ask the scared part of you to join you in this safe place. Talk to that part about coming here anytime it is afraid. Make a commitment that you will consciously come to this safe place if the scared one needs it.

TAKING STOCK

Retreat to your safe place is in no way a defeat. It is a retreat in the best sense of that word—you know, those get-away-from-the-world places? Retreat is a time to take stock, to go inside, to rest, to regroup and to be with just yourself. Take advantage of it anytime the work feels too intense. Practice using it; don't use it only as a last resort. This is not a marathon. There is not a finish line. The rewards and prizes come all the time as we do the work. The better you get at using your safe place, the more work you will get done. It has to do with being gentle with yourself, not forcing things, taking the work at your own pace. It is giving yourself permission to do it your way!

Self care is an essential part of what we are learning. Perhaps you have already received that message! Our attention now turns to using (or developing) our own internal capacity for self care in a deep and healing way.

Chapter 14
THE NURTURER

I have referred to a nurturing part several times. It is someone nice to know. Do you know this part of you? If you are a mother or father and know you nurture your children, then you do have this part. If you find it easy to give reassurance and support to friends and family, that is probably the Nurturer (although there are many other names you can use, I'll use this one). Many people have very kind and loving Nurturers who appear spontaneously to take care of other people, but rarely get the benefit of that kind of nurturing themselves. If you are going to be gentle with yourself, you need to energize the Nurturer. (If this whole concept sounds foreign to you and/or you know for sure you have no nurturing part, hang in there. I will speak to that issue in Session 10 (b). Read through this but skip the dialogue assignment.)

SESSION TEN (A)—GETTING TO KNOW THE NURTURER

If a Nurturer has not shown up yet in the exploration of your selves, do a little "search and find" mission right now. Ask: "Who cuddles my children/grandchildren? Who gladly offers support and love to friends? Who feels compassion for the victims of the world? Who offers a tissue, makes chicken soup, or a cup of tea for a hurting friend or family member?"

If you know this part well after all, you might be ready to dialogue. If it feels vague and shadowy, take some time to flesh out this part. Close your eyes and imagine the Nurturer in front of you. What is it wearing? How old is it? What is its gender? Ask all those questions from Chapter 2, Session One, page 10. In your imagination, walk around the part, move close to it and then back off. How does it feel to be close? further away? If you feel ready, ask it if it is willing to talk to you. You can either dialogue in imagery or in your journal. The advantage to the journal is you will have a "hard copy" for later reference. If you choose to dialogue in imagery, take notes in your journal when you are through.

You may be having trouble getting a clear sense of the Nurturer. It may appear but keeps slipping away. If that is happening to you, ask: "Who does not like the Nurturer? Who won't let me have access to this part?" Dialogue in your journal with that part. Remember to honor it and allow yourself to uncover the positive intent of this part. Ask it "What is your purpose? What do you think will happen if I get to know the Nurturer? What do you think will happen if the Nurturer gets more air time in my life? Can we negotiate?"

Example: *A person who is having trouble getting to the nurturer asks who is blocking:*

s: *Who doesn't want me to talk to the Nurturer?*

Part: *ME!*

s: *And who are you?*

Part: *I am your Cool Dude.*

s: *Ah, I think I may have seen you before.*

Cool Dude (CD): *Yeah, so?*

s: *How old are you CD?*

CD: *What's it to you?*

s: *Just asking. I just want to get to know you.*

CD: *Maybe I don't want to be known.*

Silence

CD: *Well, I'm 16. So?*

s: *OK. And what is it about this Nurturer part that you don't like?*

CD: *Just don't that's all.*

s: *I'm just trying to get acquainted with her. Is there some harm in that? What do you think would happen if the Nurturer talked to me?*

CD: *Don't know. Don't care! I just don't want to, okay?*

s: *Well, no it is not okay. I am trying to move forward here and I feel like you are in the way.*

CD: *So I don't like wimps!*

s: *Is the Nurturer a wimp?*

CD: *Not her.*

s: *Then who?*

CD: *That sniveling little kid.*

s: *Oh? What sniveling little kid?*

CD: *The one who wants to sit on the Nurturer's lap, that's who!*

s: *Ah. And if the little kid sits on the Nurturer's lap, then what might happen?*

CD: *That kid'll cry that's what. I hate that. What's to cry about?*

s: *I see. You are afraid the little kid will come out and she will cry.*

CD: *Yeah!*

s: *Well, CD, the way I see it, the little kid might need a lap. She might cry but she might also get comforted. I like that idea.*

CD: *Well, I don't!*

s: *I hear you. I get it. But, you know, I want to let the Nurturer talk anyway. I want to let her comfort the little kid if that is what needs to happen. I appreciate your concern but I think it will be all right.*

CD: *Whatever!*

Occasionally a part will stand steadfastly in the way. You may have to acknowledge it and move on. Because we all have a will and can make choices, you can choose whether you are going to allow a part to continue to block you.

Moving on will always go more smoothly if you have given some time to the subpersonality who is doing the blocking. It is important to listen and to honor the intent of that part. You may want to say you will take small steps in the direction you wish to go, letting the Blocking One (BO) know what you are planning and assuring it of your intention to go slowly. For example, you might start by just sitting with the Nurturer for a little while. Make note of your observations about this experience. Go back to the Blocking One (BO) and see how it feels about the experience. Now try asking just one question of the Nurturer and letting it have one short speech. Again check in with BO. This is being gentle with a part of yourself, not forcing change but easing into it, moving ahead even when a part of you is afraid.

I remember once talking to the thirteen-year-old part of a client. She was a rather obnoxious kid—as thirteen-year-olds tend to be! She was firmly entrenched and had no intention of cooperating with the adult part of my client or with me. Finally, after acknowledging her as best I could, I moved to the adult part and said, "I think you need to decide if you are going to let this kid continue to run your life." The adult self chose to reclaim control from the teenager and began making grown-up decisions about changes she wanted to make.

SESSION TEN (B)—WHEN THERE IS NO NURTURER

I promised to come back to those of you who do not feel the energy of a nurturing part at all. If none of the discussion above evoked this part, you may need to create it. Establishing a part that did not previously exist is an idea we have not yet explored. Most often when the nurturing part is absent, it is because the person had inadequate nurturance as an infant and young child. There are many reasons this can happen—none of them mean it is your fault or that there is something wrong with you. Sometimes the mother (who usually provides a preponderance of the nurturing) was absent, physically or mentally ill, or chemically dependent. If no other adult takes over the nurturing role, the child receives so little nurturance there is no model for this behavior or feeling.

Are you beginning to feel this is you? Then let's talk about how to create an "ideal model" of a nurturing part. What are the qualities you would expect to find in a nurturing parent? Make a list. Do you know someone who seems to embody these qualities? If not, make someone up! Imagine yourself having an interaction with that person and being the recipient of the things on your list. You may need to dialogue with parts of you that are protesting. Suggest that they act as if this could work and see what happens. If there is a part of you that is really scared, you may need to take the time to do some more work with that part. If you feel immobilized, don't be surprised. This is a tough thing to move past. Reread the preceding paragraphs about how to work through blocks. This is just a block.

Example: *Someone's list of nurturing qualities might look like this:*

• *loving*	• *caring*	• *soft*
• *rocking*	• *kind*	• *interested*
• *gentle*	• *listening*	• *empathic*

This person might remember a grandmother who had these qualities or perhaps a teacher. Or they might just imagine someone— choosing how that person would look, feel, act.

When you feel ready, try again to imagine yourself with the person who is nurturing and allow yourself to be nurtured. Take it in small steps over several days if need be. You have lived your whole life up till now without this part, you can afford the time it takes to let this happen.

Continuing example: *My nurturer is my grandmother. She is large and bosomy and she likes to hold me close. I can feel myself sitting on her lap in a rocker and rocking me gently. We just sit* *and rock and she croons to me, singing softly into my hair. I feel warm and safe and soothed. I know she has all the qualities on my list. I can feel her caring, her love, her gentleness. I rest in her arms.*

What are the things you want to hear from the nurturing part you have created? Make a list.

Example: *A list of* **nurturing** *statements:*

> *I love you.*
>
> *You are precious to me.*
>
> *I will hold you and soothe you when you are hurting.*
>
> *You are special to me and I will always care for you.*
>
> *I can't always keep you safe but I will always be there when you need consoling.*

Here, sit on my lap and rest your head on my bosom. I love you.
[my head is lovingly stroked and I hear crooning, soft noises
against my head.]

Spend some time with your nurturer. As you interact with the nurturing person of your imagination, allow the two of you to be surrounded with white light. The light descends and surrounds you both. You can feel it as healing, integrating energy. As the light embraces you and the nurturing person, allow that person to become one with you. Feel yourself acquiring the nurturing qualities from your list. As you and the original nurturer separate, still surrounded by the light, you can feel the qualities in yourself. Allow the image to fade and reconnect to yourself in your chair, aware of the room you are sitting in, sounds in the background, your feet on the floor. Make an entry in your journal about this experience.

Now imagine the nurturing part of yourself that you have just acquired stepping outside of your body and standing apart. Notice it and pay attention to how it looks. Experiment with being closer and further from it. Step into it (like we did in the circle and two parts exercise back in Chapter 10, Session Seven page 61). Let yourself feel "being" the part. Then step back into yourself and look at the part again. Ask: "Are you willing to talk with me?" Open your journal and begin a dialogue. If other parts show up, see if they will subside at your request. If not, you may need to talk to them. But don't give up on the Nurturer. The more you dialogue with it, the more established it will become.

USING THE NURTURER

Let's resume this nurturer work with those of you who had a nurturer from the start and those who created one. Everyone needs to talk to the nurturing part on a regular basis. It will keep this energy present and readily available to you.

Recall an incident from fairly recent events when you felt small and vulnerable. There are lots of different ways we behave when this feeling is present. Sometimes we withdraw, or become angry, or make silly jokes. See if you can allow yourself to be back in that scene. As you watch yourself, stop the action, move yourself away from the scene, place the Nurturer near you and start the action again. Allow yourself to receive caring from the Nurturer. Let the Nurturer hold you, soothe you, stroke your head, give you a cool drink—whatever feels right and good for you. Let yourself really take it all in. Feel soothed and comforted. Thank the Nurturer. Stop the action, remove the Nurturer and place your self back in the scene. Start the action again and see how it turns out. Write in your journal about this experience.

TAKING STOCK

How are you doing? We have added some parts now. Go back to your map, the drawing with the self in the middle and the parts in ovals branching out like spokes of a wheel from page 42. Fill in the subpersonalities that you have recognized now. Add the qualities of these parts. You should have a Nurturer and a Controller/Protector along with any others you have found.

How do you feel when you look at your map? Is there a sense of "knowing" as you study it? Does it all feel sort of strangely familiar? If not, don't give up! If you are getting some dialogue, you're doing fine. Familiarity is that "recognition reflex" we talked about earlier. Read the dialogues you have so far and be sure you have all the parts who have talked on your map.

Going back in your journal to read dialogue is very helpful. I usually read mine when I am finished writing and then again in the next day or two. Every now and then I go back to old dialogues to check out awareness that I had captured and that has perhaps faded. I find it helpful to highlight the lines that seem particularly important or insightful. I use two colors, one for insights and one for action steps needed.

Do you feel like you are really getting the hang of this? If not, keep practicing! Choose simple dilemmas and ask "Who has something to say about this?" Choose a subpersonality and ask it to talk to you. Ask how it operates in your life. Experiment with stepping into that part and back out again. Often the best way to truly "know" a part is to become it for a few moments and to feel the shift in energy when you move from it back to center. In the Appendix on pages 133 and 135 you will find two exercises, The Bus and The Room which provide guided imagery experiences to get in touch with parts and spend time with them. You may want to try those.

The next three chapters are probably the hardest work. I hope they are also the most rewarding. You may be slowing down the pace now as you do this deeper work. Take lots of time and space in your journal as Chapter 15 moves you on. And review your safe place—just in case you need it.

Chapter 15
DEEPENING THE WORK

You may already be working at a very deep level. Sometimes this just takes off and it has a life of its own. Maybe you don't think you need this section. Isn't that the beauty of reading a "how to" book? You can skip anything you want. If you go to a class or workshop, you are stuck with what the presenter thinks you need next! So look it over and decide whether you want to do this part. You could even be finished and we'll excuse you! But keep the dialogue going.

If you want to learn to go deeper into yourself, you probably need to make connection with the part of you that is vulnerable and afraid.

Session Eleven—The Vulnerable Child

If you are willing, let's try some work with a vulnerable part of you. This is often a child. For our purposes here, I am going to assume it is a child. You may have to substitute other words if your vulnerable part (or the one you want to work with here) is an adult.

First, identify this subpersonality. Is it already on your map? Do whatever you think is required to have a clear sense of this part (use the ways we have discussed in earlier sections). Add it to your map if it is not already there.

Now check in with the Controller/Protector. After acknowledging the CP, ask how it feels about your dialoguing with the Vulnerable Child (VC). Ask if it has any limits it wants to place on this work. Tell it you honor its role in protecting you and that if anything that happens makes it feel uncomfortable, you would appreciate it showing up to talk to you directly about that. It is my experience that the CP will divert you anyway if it doesn't like what is happening. It is an advantage to have it appear and talk with you because then you know what the issue is, why there is a block here. You don't walk away from the dialogue feeling sort of incomplete and not knowing why.

Example: A dialogue with the CP might look like this:

self(s): *CP, how are you feeling about my talking to VC?*

CP: *Nervous.*

s: *Tell me about that.*

CP: *It feels a little dangerous to me. Remember, you energize parts you talk to?*

s: *That is true. But I think the VC needs to speak.*

CP: *Probably. But you might feel really little and really vulnerable. I like to keep you safe from those kinds of feelings.*

s: *I know you do. And you do a wonderful job. But I think you and the Nurturer and I can take care of this child all right.*

CP: *I suppose.*

s: *Tell you what! How about if we let this child come and speak and if you get too nervous about it, you just come back and tell me and we'll see where to go next?*

CP: *Sounds okay to me.*

s: *Thanks, CP.*

Now begin the dialogue with the VC. An early question needs to be "How old are you?" This helps you to ask appropriate questions. If the child is preverbal (not so likely in this kind of dialogue on paper but it does happen), then you need to just be with it for awhile. By this I mean, sit with the small child, imagining it before you (or in your arms). You can talk to it but don't ask questions or expect verbal responses. Try to convey your respect and unconditional love by your presence rather than by an exchange of words. Then let an older part talk about the experience of that child.

Once when I was doing my own Voice Dialogue work with a therapist, a six week old part of me showed up! All I could do was be with her. Then an older child came and talked about the baby's experience. My grandmother died when I was six weeks old and my very tiny child part wanted me to know how scary that was. She felt like it was her job to comfort our mother and that was overwhelming!

As you talk to the young child, keep your language appropriate. Don't use big words that a child this age would not understand. Don't ask deep, philosophical questions. Children often don't know "why"— not why they behave a certain way, and certainly not why they feel a certain way. Ask the child to tell you about itself, how it feels, what it wants, what it needs. Often children mostly want to know they are loved. They want you to pay attention to them. Often they are parts that have received a lot of criticism and rejection (from *you* as well as from the outside world). Your job is to listen and offer comfort and reassurance.

A Personal Story: I used to be very afraid of heights. I was also a white-knuckle flyer. I never stayed home because I was afraid to fly, but rather I dreaded the flight and was tense and uncomfortable until it was over— hearing every nuance of the plane's engine and feeling flooded with fear every time it hit turbulence. My husband loved flying and had a life-long dream of being a pilot. A short time before we were to go to Hawaii for the first time, he got his private pilot's license. So I had a double reason to get over my fear of flying: I didn't want to miss his joy of flying a small plane, and I didn't want to spend a wonderful vacation worrying about the next time I had to get on a plane (to say nothing of a solid nine hours in the air to get there!!).

My first step in recovery was to develop a hierarchy of my fears—from the least scary part (1) to the most terrifying (10). This helped me realize that the worst thing was not so likely to happen and that there were many gradations in my fear. Then I asked myself the question, "If I allowed myself to get over being afraid, what might happen?" This question let me know that I had a choice (The Will, remember?—that magic phrase "allowed myself" is the key). I also discovered what I was unconsciously gaining from holding onto my fear. It had to do with excuses for not expanding my horizons and with needing reassurance but not feeling I was entitled to it. There is more about this in the next section.

Then I asked, "Who is afraid?" You are probably not surprised to hear it was a child. She is five and her name is Jeanie. Her mommy always said, "Don't be afraid." Mommy meant well. But Jeanie says she felt afraid anyway and then didn't think there was anyone who would listen. She wanted me to love her and to hold her hand. She needed reassurance that I would be there, that it is not being bad to be afraid. I promised her that when we were on the big plane to Hawaii, I would hold her hand. I told her this was a scary thing to do but that it would be okay. I honored her and her fear and her needs.

Not only did I make it to Hawaii with ease, I rode a helicopter into the mountains with only one brief moment of near terror (well, the pilot swooped around so those on the other side could see and it was quite a dip and swirl maneuver!) Jeanie held my hand but she loved seeing rainbows in the rainiest place in the world and beautiful waterfalls tumbling down the mountain sides.

This work with Jeanie also relieved my fear of high places. I was able to descend an open grilled fire escape at work that had always terrified me. I went with my husband in his small plane. On our first long trip, I even decided that my tension probably wasn't what was holding the plane up and so I completely relaxed! Now I fly and climb to high places with no fear at all. Jeanie still needs me for other situations, but rarely when it comes to flying or a scenic look out.

SOME WORDS ABOUT RESISTANCE

You have probably heard the word "resistance" used in psychological jargon even if you are not in therapy or a therapist. I have often thought it the most maligned word in the therapeutic repertoire. The problem is we are all inclined to think of it as a negative thing. Resistance is not "bad," it is natural. We all resist change, new things, letting go. Usually, if we examine ourselves (like with dialogue for instance!) we discover that there has been a good reason to resist the change. That does not mean the change doesn't need to happen, just that some part or parts of us have reasons to hold onto what they already know.

An example can be found in my fear of flying and heights story. When I asked myself the "If I allowed myself" question, what I learned was that I was afraid I couldn't hack it if I let go of the fear. If everyone knew I was afraid of heights, no one would expect me to climb the look out tower and I didn't have to risk failing. My boss walked down the front stairs with me and never expected me to use the fire escape route to our cars, so I didn't have to risk getting midway down and going to pieces. What if I wasn't afraid of flying and my husband expected me to just go flying off with him any old time? Then what if I did, and in mid-flight I had a panic attack because I was so afraid? If I was afraid to fly, no one would expect me to go in a small plane or to fly any unnecessary flights—like helicopters to sight see! And all of this doesn't even mention that it gave me some measure of attention, "specialness." Ugh. But it is true!

I had to recognize what there was to gain by keeping my fears. Then I had to make a choice to let go of them before any work I did was going to be effective. When we get what we want, we usually have to give up something. I wanted to be unafraid but I had to give up the excuses, the safety from risk, and the specialness to get there.

Before we can give something up or make a change, we often have to know what the motivation for keeping it the same is (or resistance!). We need to make the shift from self-criticism to self-acceptance.

When you read my story about Jeanie being afraid, did you get mad at her? Did you ridicule her; think she was dumb or silly? Probably not. Your nurturing part probably smiled benignly and said, "ooh, honey..." But when you encounter your own resistance, I am willing to bet you are not so kind and sympathetic. Most of us are inclined to think of ourselves as bad, wrong, dumb, or silly when we are afraid to change something.

It is time to call up the "be gentle with yourself" phrase again. You need to learn to afford yourself the same kindness and patience you would afford someone else. When we accept ourselves, we understand that we are just acting like a human being! We can let every part have its say and can redirect our Critic. Critics can be very helpful when it comes to evaluating situations, discernment, weighing options. They are almost always pure destruction when turned on ourselves.

I could not help Jeanie get past her fears until I accepted and honored her. I would never have been able to reassure her if I was telling her, "Bad girl, just behave and don't cause trouble." I had to tell myself that it is normal to be afraid, that having a little girl inside who is scared is not being weak or bad.

TAKING STOCK

How are you doing with the vulnerable child idea? I have to confess I am a little nervous. My wonderful daughter/reader was skeptical. She said, "I never would have thought there was a child part of me. I don't know about this part." To me it felt like she was saying, "No one is going to buy this one, Mom!"

If it didn't just flow for you either, let's look at it a little more. Don't you sometimes feel a lot younger than your chronological age? Maybe your boss yells at you. You 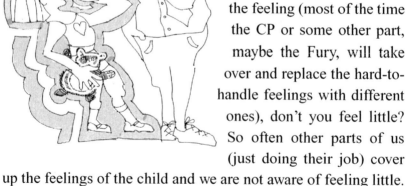 feel shame or anger or both. Maybe you are in a situation that makes you feel afraid or not good enough. Maybe someone talks down to you. If you really let yourself sink into the feeling (most of the time the CP or some other part, maybe the Fury, will take over and replace the hard-to-handle feelings with different ones), don't you feel little? So often other parts of us (just doing their job) cover up the feelings of the child and we are not aware of feeling little.

It is my experience that when we explore it further, most people can identify a child part. We think all of us has grown up, but the child is still there. We are every age we have ever been. We carry the experience of ourselves in the past with us in the present. In a workshop, Hal Stone once said that he doesn't think the child ever grows up. Roberto Assagioli would probably say this part can transform. I don't know if he meant it would grow up. I know I still have that little five year old child but she is not nearly so afraid. She knows I will comfort her and help her and she lets me know she needs me. I think that is transformation. So maybe Hal and Roberto are saying the same thing. That is a new idea to me.

Now we will move from the light into the dark. We take a look next at parts of us we often deny. We will learn to recognize their value as well as ways to harness their energy.

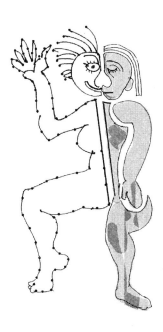

Chapter 16
THE DARK SIDE

There is a part of me (it is my critic part who I call the Commanding Officer or CO) who is saying, "Okay, now you are going to get yourself into trouble. Nobody wants to hear about this. Why don't you quit while you are ahead?" Well, for one thing I don't even know if I *am* ahead! And for another, I don't know how we can talk about self-acceptance and skip the concept of the shadow or dark side.

We probably need a definition here. When I refer to the dark side or shadow (I'll use these terms interchangeably), I am talking about the side of us that is not interested in goodness and light. Freud called it "id." It is primitive and self-centered. It wants its needs met *now* and doesn't care who suffers to provide. It even sometimes wishes other people harm! It can be mean and mean-spirited. It will take and take and never give.

Do you know who I mean? Or are you telling yourself, "She isn't talking about me. I don't have any part or parts like that?"

Let me see. Does that mean you have never been jealous and withheld a compliment or a tip because of it? You've never finished the last of the chocolate pie in the refrigerator when you knew you had your share and your spouse was counting on having it after work? You have never said a spiteful word or— well, I suspect you are getting the picture. The Shadow. The Dark Side. How are we ever going to love and honor that in us? Perhaps a better question is, "How will we ever know true self-acceptance if we do not honor even *that* in us?"

Self-acceptance is being able to say, "Ah yes, there is that in me. I have been selfish, mean, aggressive, jealous, querulous, obnoxious." It is acknowledging it, owning it, understanding that it means we are human. Does it give us license to hurt others? No, of course not. But it does mean accepting the shadow as a part of us, forgiving ourselves, making reparation where necessary, and moving on.

In an effort to teach children right from wrong and socially acceptable behavior, adults often send a very confusing message. When a child says, "I hate you!" we say, "We don't hate people. You don't hate your brother. We all love each other." What does that mean to the child about the rageful feeling inside? Probably it means, "I am a bad person because what I am feeling is not acceptable, normal, human." These early messages are the beginning of the denial of the shadow-side of our nature.

SESSION TWELVE—NEW MESSAGES

This is a good time to get out your journal and ask yourself what messages you received as a child about your own shadow. Jot down the negative messages. You might want to write several paragraphs about what this felt like for you as a child. Now write counter messages—new meanings to old events. Some examples:

Old Message: Hate is bad. I am bad because I feel rage and hate.
New Message: Hate and rage are emotions that are human. These emotions only mean that I am human. I can choose how I am going to feel about the event that triggered these emotions and about how I am going to behave.

Old Message: It is wrong to feel jealous about my friend's new dress.
New Message: Jealousy is a normal human emotion. I really wish I had a new dress, too. I can choose how I am going to feel and behave about this.

Did you notice how in these examples I used the words "emotion" and "feeling" as if they are two different things? We tend to use these words interchangeably but I have come to realize they are not the same. At least for the purpose of our mutual understanding can we assume they are not? Let's try new definitions.

I'd like to define "emotion" as a visceral (in the body) reaction to an event and "feeling" as what we make up about that reaction. My boss criticized me with angry words that sent a wave of shock and recoil through me. That was the raw emotion. I had an array of feelings I could decide to have about this event. I could choose to feel furious, outraged, offended, unjustly berated, hurt, inadequate, unacceptable...we could go on and on. Or I could choose to feel okay with myself. I could look at my actions, decide if I needed to change something or make reparations in some way and if so, do that. I could recognize that the anger was really my boss's and that I did not *have* to feel anything about who I am in response to that anger.

Self-acceptance—accepting the dark side of human nature, of our own nature, may seem counter to being a good person. You will need to look closely at the messages you received as a child about being a good person and make adult choices about what you really believe. Guilt for our harmful actions against others is healthy guilt. Guilt for who we are is not healthy.

Does it seem we are getting way too psychological here? Perhaps. But if you don't look at some of the messages you received and decide how you feel about them now, you will continue to say to your inner child the same destructive things that were said when you were actually a child. It is the same principle we see operating when we find ourselves saying things to our children that we swore we would never say because we know how much they hurt us when our parents said them. We tend to repeat what we know until we make an adult decision to do something new.

In her book, *The Artist's Way*, Julia Cameron (see the Reference Section) calls the negative messages "blurts." She says we need to answer every blurt with an affirmation. I think that is a good practice. And believe me it *takes* practice. In case affirmations are new to you, they are the "new messages" in my example. It is important not to use negative words. In an affirmation we say, "I can" and "I will" instead of "I can't" and "I won't." Words that are any form of "not" or "no" do not belong in an affirmation. It can be tricky to get that right. In the second new message example above, it is tempting to say "I don't have to feel jealous about that." But that breaks the rule. Say instead, "I can choose how I am going to feel about that."

We've gone down this path because we need tools if we are going to change behaviors that trip us up. Often we need new words to say to our parts. Sometimes that means whole new ideas. If it is a new idea to you to affirm yourself, play with it and see how wonderful it feels.

SESSION THIRTEEN—YOUR SHADOW

So now back to your own dark side. Ask yourself, "Who?" (What part of me?) This is always the question, "Who?" There may be more than one part here. If you are willing and feel ready, allow yourself to explore this issue. What parts of you are difficult to own, to look at, to accept? Who carries the shadow for you?

I have a part I've introduced to you before in one of the sample dialogues. I call it "The Fury." The Fury is not interested in serving anyone's interests. It is a part that is angry and fiery and selfish. I did not meet this part in early dialogue work. But it has been very helpful to hear its voice. If you have the courage, try some dialogue with whoever shows up when you ask, "Who?" You may need to start with seeing the part and fleshing it out as we have done before. Add the part or parts you discover to your map. Now ask who is the opposite or polarity to this part. Let that part talk, too. It is not a good idea to energize the shadow parts without countering that energy with a more constructive one. Make it a rule to always talk to a positive part after you talk to a shadow part.

Example: *I see The Fury as dark and fiery red at the same time. It wears a red and black cape and swoops around almost cackling. In my art journal this part is represented by a costume in a parade that is a phoenix, I think—a great red bird with bright feathers.*

self (s): *Fury will you talk here for a moment?*

Fury (F): *What for?*

s: *I am just trying to demonstrate for these folks how a part like you looks and sounds.*

F: *Well, I don't want to be bothered.*

s: *You are the part of me that carries anger, am I right?*

F: *So?*

s: *So I know you don't feel you get the air time you would like or the respect you need.*

F: *That's true enough.*

s: *Tell me more about that.*

F: *Well, too many of your parts are wimps. Everybody just clams up. I want to let the world know how I feel; I want to shout from the roof tops—really loud! You are always telling me to cool it. I am not cool. I am fiery and angry and loud!*

s: *Sometimes I am glad to have you around. You do speak my truth sometimes when it needs to be spoken. You demand my needs be addressed. You put me first.*

F: *Yep. That's me. Only I'd do a lot more of it if I had my way!*

s: *Well, I appreciate your availability. We'll talk again sometime soon.*

F: *Sure, cut me off for "those folks" you're trying to teach. I didn't come out to please them—or you for that matter.*

s: *Thanks all the same, Fury.*

F: *Yeah, whatever!*

A good counter energy for me is the Maskless Me. She is so well-grounded and centered that she is able to handle the energy of the Fury.

self (s): *MM will you say a few words here?*

Maskless Me (MM): *Always. It is important to acknowledge Fury. This is not a bad part of you. I am always close at hand to see that things don't get too destructive out there in the real world.*

s: *Yes, I know. And I appreciate that. I think sometimes I suppress Fury too much because I am afraid of what might happen if its energy is unleashed.*

MM: *Yes. I think that is an accurate assessment. Remember to let Fury speak and to honor its anger. You can always make the choices about what you are going to do. And you can always call on me to help you.*

s: *Thanks. I'll remember that.*

The second dialogue helps me get back to my center and not hold on to the unrest of the Fury. It provides the countering I mentioned at the end of the paragraph preceding this dialogue–reconnecting with constructive energy.

TAKING STOCK

We have probably just dealt with the hardest part. Do you feel a little dark having talked to this part (or if you didn't yet, listening to mine)? The shadow is probably the most denied energy. People feel afraid of it. In my first class using the first draft of this book, a student wanted me to change the name. This student felt very uncomfortable with "the dark side" label. I considered a change of language. Then I rejected that idea. It seems then I would be supporting the notion that this is something to be avoided, glossed over, sugar-coated. Instead I want us to be able to look at it out in the light, unguilded, naked.

It may take some time before you are able to fully own your own shadow energy. I know I am still working on it! Be patient with yourself but please don't write off this chapter. It is an important one. If you are having trouble identifying your own dark side part or parts, try talking to other parts about this. Ask who is not wanting to acknowledge the shadow part. Don't forget to ask: "Who is the opposite of the shadow?" You may want to talk to that part. It may have some insight into the shadow. It will also gain energy and make you feel more confident that you can come back to the positive energy—you will not get lost in your dark side.

Next we're going to get to know our critical part better. I am sure it is not a stranger to you even if you have not yet talked to it. If this is a strong voice, you may feel some trepidation. You have come so far! Don't bail out now! Hint: You may recognize someone here you know or have known outside of yourself.

Chapter 17
THE CRITIC

We have talked about the critic part several times. This is such an important part that Hal Stone has written a whole book about it! (See Reference Section: Stone, Hal. *Embracing Your Inner Critic*.) Getting a book all its own has probably added to its tendency toward pomposity!

Do you have a critic part on your map? I've told you my critic is called Commanding Officer and that he wears white gloves and inspects everything. He is also a perfectionist.

If you haven't identified the part of you that criticizes and judges, you should take time to do so deliberately. This is a part of us that can get in the way of moving forward. It can tear us down and create depression. Sometimes the critic part is loud and obvious and sometimes it is devious and subtle. Your critic might be all of these things or have only one aspect. Either way it is important to learn about the critic part and know when it is active.

When I am going to teach a class or a workshop, my CO often gets going. Sometimes I just feel a stirring in my belly. I realize I am worried and it is showing up in my insides. My body is aware but my conscious mind is not. That is when I sit down to journal and find out what is going on. I want to go into my presentation feeling centered and able to connect with the people who want to hear what I have to say. I can't do that if the CO is making me nervous and telling me I am inadequate. If we talk, we can almost always work things out!

Example: A discussion with my CO might look like this:

s: *CO, are you the one giving me a hard time about this presentation?*

Commanding Officer (CO): *Well, you have to admit you have barely prepared!*

s: *But, CO, I know this stuff.*

CO: *So what? To do a really spectacular job you have to work at it. When I listen to other people talk about all the time they put into presenting, I am appalled at what a slacker you are.*

s: *I think I usually do okay.*

CO: *OKAY?! Okay is not good enough—not by a long shot. You need to be a lot better than okay. You need to be excellent. You need to look good.*

s: *Well, CO, I think maybe those are your needs. I appreciate it when you help me get things together. You have good ideas. But I don't want to spend too much time on preparation for things I feel I already know how to do. After all, CO, we are choosing only to* *do things we already know these days. Much of the success of the presentation has to do with connecting with the audience and addressing their specific interests or needs.*

CO: *Well, you still need to be good! You waste time and fiddle around doing things that aren't as important when you could be preparing. You could write an outline, make more handouts, DO something!*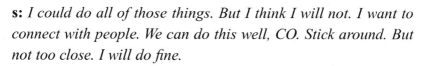

s: *I could do all of those things. But I think I will not. I want to connect with people. We can do this well, CO. Stick around. But not too close. I will do fine.*

Maskless Me: *Yes! Don't succumb to his need to do it perfectly. Perfection can look slick and canned and not promote relationships. People will learn from you because you connect, not because you are perfect.*

s: *Thanks, MM, I needed to hear that!*

So whether you want to or not, open that journal and learn about your critic. Find out what it is like and how it operates, whether it is overworked, what it needs to be willing to back off a little. Remember even the Critic has to be honored and appreciated. It is often the part of us that gives us the gift of discernment. You wouldn't really want to be without it. It also can be a parental voice that you heard as a child. Whenever you are feeling shame, embarrassment, discouragement, performance anxiety, your critic may be close at hand. A dialogue will help you sort it out and figure out how to get centered and move forward. Ask the

Critic how it helps you out. Some of the ways it claims are a help, you may see as a detriment. But you may be surprised at how it does help you. Regardless, it needs to be honored.

TAKING STOCK

How are you doing? I didn't lose you when I started that shadow talk did I? Do you see how important acceptance and honoring are? In my work as a therapist and educator/supervisor of therapists, I have watched this dynamic operate in many ways. It seems to me we change best from a place of feeling honored and accepted. We may have to feel enough pain in the place we *are*, to make it worth taking the risks (and let's face it, often they are considerable) to change something. But unless somehow we can enter an environment (or create one as we have been doing here) that makes us feel relatively safe, we often stay very stuck.

The last two chapters have taken us to places we often avoid. How has that been for you? You might want to journal about the experience of looking at your dark side and your critic. Give yourself lots of credit for the work you have done here. Most of us work on all of our parts for a life-time. But especially the shadow parts have to be returned to again and again. We have to keep drawing on our courage to take a peek, then a deeper look. Even though I've told you all the parts are trying to help you, it is hard to keep that in mind. You have to be gentle with yourself over and over again. You have to persistently dialogue to work things out with the parts that seem to be working against you. I believe that you will always, eventually, come to understand their needs. They will demonstrate their willingness to work with you. Then you'll come to trust the process and be less likely to avoid addressing them.

Do you feel the last assignments have taken you to a deeper place? Are you finding yourself thinking of doing the dialogue on your own (instead of following what the next step in the book is)? That, of course, is our ultimate goal. I must admit here that sometimes I will struggle with an issue for weeks before I hit myself in the head and say, "How about dialogue?" So don't be discouraged if you haven't been finding yourself running to your journal without prompting. But do try to find ways to remind yourself of this tool.

I find that discipline is hard to come by for me. When I read *The Artist's Way*, Julia Cameron reminded me of the benefits of regular journaling. She recommends three pages every single morning—"morning pages" she calls them. I used to do journaling nearly every day but had moved away from it. At Julia's prompting, I started again and it has helped me remember to dialogue, too. You may want to try it.

You are getting to the home stretch. We will look a little more closely at the idea of the transpersonal or higher unconscious in the last chapter. Then all that is left is some ideas for continuing work. Turn the page!

Chapter 18
FINAL THOUGHTS

We have talked about using dialogue to resolve dilemmas. We've used it to understand ourselves and our motivations more clearly. Hopefully you have found ways to use it to work out stuck places in your life. When I look back at all the chapters, I am impressed that you have stayed with me! If you've been writing all along you have done a considerable amount of work.

While I was swimming one day (laps, so lots of time to think), I suddenly had this flash: *But you haven't addressed the idea of spirituality!* It is true. I've only referred to the fact that Assagioli posits the existence of the Transpersonal Self and says we have stored things in the higher unconscious as well as the lower.

The thing that drew me to psychosynthesis in the first place was that it added the spiritual dimension which is often over looked in psychology. An addictions counselor I talked with recently told me the longer she works in the field, the more convinced she is that no one gets better without connecting to the spiritual. Often these days I hear people talking about our spiritual deprivation. Then I was going to just gloss over it!

So I had to go back and say, "Who? What do I know about the part of me that keeps me from remembering to talk about what I know is so important?" It is a nine year old. I'll call her Jean (J). Here's what she has to say:

s: *J, tell me what is up?*

J: *Well, I think it is better if you don't talk about stuff that sometimes makes people mad.*

s: *Oh, you think it makes people mad to talk about the spiritual side of things?*

J: *Sure. Especially about religion, beliefs, God—that kind of stuff.*

s: *I see. Well, that is the beauty of psychosynthesis. You don't have to talk about religion or doctrine or God even. You can talk about being connected to that which is outside of the self in anyway that makes the person feel comfortable.*

J: *Yeah? And people won't get mad?*

s: *No, sweetie. I don't find that people get mad. Especially if they have been reading this whole book. If they were going to get mad, I think they would have done that long ago.*

J: *Maybe you are right. Some people probably did get mad. I didn't think I would like you writing a book. But sometimes it has been easier for me than when you talk. At least we won't know who got mad at us now.*

s: *That's true. Are you the part who keeps coming in to ask if people are still with us?*

J: *I guess. I just don't want anybody mad at us.*

s: *What do you think would happen if people got mad at us?*

J: *They wouldn't like me.*

s: *And if they don't like you?*

J: *Well that feels bad. I like people to like me.*

s: *It isn't likely that everyone will like you.*

J: *I don't want to know that. I know how to make people not get mad.*

s: *How's that?*

J: *Don't talk about stuff they might not like. Like spiritual stuff.*

s: *I see.*

J: *So are you gonna write about this stuff?*

s: *I don't know yet what to say. But I think I have to write about it.*

J: *I'm gonna hide!*

s: *Okay. You can hide. I'll let other parts do the writing and you don't have to peek if anybody gets mad.*

J: *Okay. But if someone does, don't blame me.*

s: *You've got it—nobody will say you did it.*

J: *Good!!*

Hopefully, that will unblock this and let me write this part. It is hard to know what to say here. I think I mostly want to suggest that all this work we are doing ties into the concept of purpose. Assagioli tells us there is a purpose for our life and that our work is about determining that purpose and living it. As you expand your self-awareness, it becomes apparent that "me" is not all there is. The more we study and read and explore, the more we realize there are connections everywhere we look. Great thinkers of all time have dealt with similar issues. They don't all come to the same conclusions but they struggle with the universal dilemmas.

As you do your work, you move the dotted lines on Assagioli's egg diagram on page 36. You enlarge the middle unconscious—the part to which you have ready access.

What does this mean in our parts work? It means that we need to give the light at least as much attention as the dark! That shadow stuff we addressed in Chapter 16 unlocked some of the lower unconscious. How can we unlock the higher unconscious?

The first step is to suggest to yourself that there is something there. The next is to say, "What do I know about the part of me that believes in spirit?" or "...the part of me that prays, meditates, feels a thrill of connection to God, the universe, other people?" It will help you to clarify your beliefs if you talk to the parts that already practice them.

As I attempt to address this business of the spiritual dimension, I am very aware of the wide variation in beliefs and attitudes about this topic. I believe we each need to find the path that works best for us. It never seems right to push my faith on my clients so I don't think it is right to push it on my readers. I do suggest that you explore what you believe and how you make important decisions about your life from your spiritual belief system. Dialoguing with different parts about how they see spirituality will give you lots of information and a place to begin examining and revising if needed.

Here are some more ideas about how to use dialogue for deeper self- understanding and to access the higher realms:

- **Dreams:** I asked earlier if you record your dreams and suggested you might try doing so. If you have a dream you can recall or have recorded, try thinking of the people, objects and events in the dream as parts of yourself. Choose one and dialogue with it. You don't need to assign a part you already know to this part of the dream. For example if you dreamed about a big house, dialogue with the house:

self (s): *House, tell me about you.*

House (H): *I represent your life. I am big and spacious and filled with light.*

s: *In my dream I was trying to find someplace in you but kept making wrong turns.*

H: *You are searching for something in your life to make it feel more complete. You keep looking outside yourself. You need to be patient and look in my many rooms.*

s: *And what will I find?*

H: *More aspects of yourself! Deeper understanding of who you are. More self-acceptance. You are always opening up new possibilities, new dimensions.*

The next step here might be to do some imagery work with the house. Explore it. Open doors. Open shades. Turn on lights. See what is there. Dialogue with objects you find, or people. Play with it.

- **People from your past:** Dialogue with a parent or friend who has died. Play both parts, yours and theirs. Ask questions you've always wanted to ask. Trust the answers. Yes, they are coming from within *you*, but they are likely to be very enlightening.

Another variation on this is to write a "letter" to this person. Say everything you have always wanted to say. Then write the letter you think that person would have written back. If it is not an affirming response, write the letter you *wish* you would have received. These two exercises can also be done with people in your present life. Never mail the letters, though! This is an internal exploration. You will confuse the relationship unless it is a very positive and supportive one already. This is not about some external reality. It is about exploring your own, internal reality.

- **Imagery with parts:** Choose a part you would like to know better or with whom you have been having difficulty. Put some music on that you like and that has no words. Sit in a comfortable chair or stretch out on the floor. Center yourself. Imagine yourself and the part together in a safe and interesting place. Take a walk on a beach or in the woods or climb a mountain. Experience this place together. Have a conversation. Exchange gifts. Imagine white light surrounding the two of you. (You don't have to do all of these things, keep them in mind, and go with the flow). Make notes in your journal about this experience.

- **Collage work:** Either in your art journal or on poster board or regular paper, create a collage for a part (or all of your parts, or some of your parts). Cut pictures and words from magazines and arrange them in ways that seem to express the part. In my art journal I have most of my parts. I have layered the pages for each part, hiding some pieces, leaving others to be gradually uncovered. To me this felt like I was expressing the sense that there was not *one* definition or "picture" that captured a part but many and that each was layered. Play. Have fun. When I read Julia Cameron's book, *The Artist's Way*, this is often what I did for my artist's date.

- **Other art modalities:** If you are artistically inclined, I don't need to tell you what medium to use or what is available. If you are not (like me!), this is a wonderful opportunity to turn off you logical mind and let yourself go. The expression of a part could end up being shapes or colors, blurs or forms. This has nothing to do with making exact replicas of anything. It has nothing to do with artistic talent. It is about freeing yourself up to let things come through unusual and less familiar  modalities. Use clay, or paint, or wood. Sculpt, finger paint, carve, whittle, cut/paste. Start with a sense of what you want to explore and then disconnect your thinking brain and let it happen. Trust that whatever shows up is exactly what is supposed to be there. When you have created something, you might want to dialogue with it in your journal. At the very least, jot down your thoughts, insights, feelings.

- **Dance:** Okay, I know for those of you, who do not consider yourselves dancers, this is a stretch. But trust me, it can be marvelous. Choose a time when you are alone and a place where you can count on privacy and have enough room to move. Let a part choose the music. Stand in the center of your space and slowly allow the part to take over your body. At first it may just be a posture you assume. Then let your body begin to move as the part. Sometimes it helps to begin with one body part (even just a finger) moving as the part. Let the part take over. Journal when you feel finished with the dance or movement. Describe the feelings and record new understandings. You might want to set up a dialogue with the part. Ask it how it felt being allowed to lead the dance.

• **Music:** If you are a musician (no matter how amateur), try letting a part play your instrument. If you sing, let a part sing. And if you are a musical klutz (like me!) try drumming. Drumming is a wonderful way for those of us with no noticeable musical abilities, to express a part. As in the dance, you can let the part take over and simply express itself. Journal when you are finished.

TAKING STOCK

Believe it or not we have been addressing the suppression of the sublime—the tendency to relegate our higher selves and transpersonal material to the higher unconscious. I'm not sure I am satisfied with leaving it here. But you do have lots of tools to work on this by now. And maybe for me to elaborate any further will take another book.

Did the suggestions here transport you to new places or turn you off? Don't tell my nine year old if you are mad! You may already have lots of wonderful ways to explore and express spirituality in your life. Sometimes a little time with nature is the ticket. Don't do what I almost did and ignore this part. And don't guilt yourself about it either. It is okay to take it slow and in little pieces. There are so many different paths where spirit is concerned. Find your own. As in all of this work, be gentle with yourself.

SUMMING UP

Wow! I feel like we have been on quite a journey together. I hope you have found it fun and exciting. Is your journal pretty full by now, lots of dialogue and other stuff? I wonder if you are finding it fun. Maybe fun is the wrong word—gratifying, helpful, exciting, challenging? Maybe it is not "fun" until a piece of work is done. Then to see what has happened, what has emerged from your unconscious—isn't it grand?

We've traveled from "beginning to know that subpersonalities, parts, energies adds a dimension to self-understanding" to "talking to our parts, learning from them, and finding creative ways to let them express themselves." If you have chosen to read the theoretical parts, you have learned about Roberto Assagioli's concept of psychosynthesis, and Hal and Sidra Stone's Voice Dialogue technique.

Hopefully one "knowing" that has evolved is that learning about oneself is a fluid process, not something with a beginning, middle and end. Now you have some new ways to work with yourself, to approach dilemmas and to explore your own depths. There is no end. We need to take delight in the process and recognize it as ongoing. Wouldn't it be boring if we "arrived?" What if we could completely "know" ourselves? Wouldn't then the adventure be gone? As you become more and more self-accepting, I think you will also become more and more excited about doing your personal growth work. Eventually, you will know that there are no nasty surprises, only more wonderful things to know and understand about yourself. We hear people talk about this work as "being on the path." But have you noticed that the path ends at the tips of your toes? You create the path as you take the next step. Keep on stepping. And walk in love.

THE APPENDIX

Contents

I. EXERCISES

In the text of this book, I promised you some exercises to help with imagery and centering. The Apple is an excellent way to get acquainted with the idea of guided imagery. Guided imagery is a technique that Assagioli used often to help clients tap into unconscious material, to work with subpersonalities, and to explore in greater depth images/symbols that came in a variety of modalities, including dreams. The Apple also engages all of your senses and helps you to understand which is more powerful for you. As was explained in the text, you can learn to substitute the sense that works for you whenever you are instructed to "see."

We will work with creating a safe place for you. Then you will know that whatever imagery work you do, you can go to your safe place to rest and recover if things get a little intense.

You may want to read these exercises onto a tape so you can close your eyes and follow the instructions. Or find a friend to trade reading with you. Use a soft, gentle voice to read aloud and go slowly. That will help you get into the light trance that allows images to flow forth. Pause for a moment at the end of each direction (especially where there are dots...) to give yourself time to "see, hear, feel, smell."

II. THE APPLE*

Imagine an apple in front of you. See its size ..., its shape ..., its color ... Is it shiny or dull? Pick it up. Feel its texture, heft, temperature ... Rub your fingers across its surface. Feel any imperfections in the skin .... Put your finger down in the stem place—is there a stem? ... Hear the squeakiness as you rub your fingers over the surface. ... Put the apple to your nose and smell it ... Bite into it ... Hear the crunch ... Feel the juiciness ... Is it crunchy, mushy, juicy, dry? ... Smell it again ... Taste it ... Be aware of its texture in your mouth ... of the taste ... Be as completely in this experience as you can, using all of your senses to experience the apple ...

When you feel finished with it, record your responses. Which sense gave you the clearest sense of the apple? If you could feel it best, that is probably the sense that makes things most accessible to you and through which you will be able to access information from the unconscious. If you can best taste, hear, smell, that sense is the one that will most quickly and completely get you into an image. Most guided imagery exercises use visual language. Now that you know what your most accessible sense is, you can substitute it for "see." You will probably get better results.

*If you hate apples, substitute a fruit or food you do like!

III. A SAFE PLACE

Sit in a comfortable chair or stretch out on the floor. It is best to have no crossed body parts. That just lets the energy flow more freely and allows your body to relax more fully. Close your eyes and take a few deep breaths. Let your body relax. Then ask yourself, "Where is a place that I feel completely safe?" You can have anything and anybody with you that will help you feel safe. You might choose a wood, a beach, your own bedroom. It can be a totally made up place/room or one you know. You may want a favorite pet, a person or to be all alone. The important thing is to have it be a place where you feel entirely safe. In imagery you can have whatever you need. If you need a weapon to feel safe, you can have it! Imagine yourself in this place where you feel safe. Use all of your senses to put yourself completely in this scene. Be aware of what you see ... Notice what you smell ... what you hear ... temperature and textures you feel. Enjoy it for a few minutes. Be aware that you can bring yourself to this place any time you need it. Remind yourself of this anytime you do imagery work.

IVA. CENTERING

Get into a comfortable position. Close your eyes. Pay attention to your breath. Don't try to regulate it, just pay attention ... to the in and the out of your breath. As you breathe, be aware that you can breathe in quiet and breathe out tension ... Forget what you know about anatomy and breathe all the way into your abdomen ... Feel the tension flow our with your breath ... Feel your muscles relax and let go ... Breathe into your legs ... all the way down to your toes. Feel the muscles smooth out and let go ... Breathe up across your shoulders and into your arms, down to your finger tips, breathing in quiet and breathing out tension ... Breathe up your neck into your scalp and your face. Letting go, feel the muscles smooth out and let go ... Breathe down your back, into your but-tocks, letting go ... Allow your body to relax, to feel quiet ... Do a check-in with your body. Breathe into any places that still feel tight or tense ... Then change your focus to your emotions. As your body is quiet you can allow your emotions to be quiet. If you have feelings that are pulling at you, that make you feel unsettled, imagine putting them one by one into little helium bal-loons and allowing them to float to the ceiling. Be aware that you can retrieve them at any time if you need them, but that for now, you are allowing them to float to the ceiling and to have your emotions be quiet ... Then as your body and your emotions are quiet, imagine your mind as a blue sky and your thoughts as puffy, white clouds floating across it. Be aware that you can allow yourself to watch the clouds pass by without attaching to any of them ... allowing your mind to be quiet ... your emotions to be quiet ... and your body to be quiet. From this quiet place, affirm your choice to allow yourself to be centered, to be quiet and in touch with your core self. Take a few moments to just "be" in this place ... Then affirm your choice to allow whatever needs to happen, to happen and proceed with whatever work you are ready to do.

Note: The above exercise moves us through the body, the emotions, and the mind as we quiet ourselves. Assagioli called these three the vehicles of expression and they were another of his "maps." Moving the quieting through each of them prepares us on three levels to do the work.

IVB. OTHER CENTERING IDEAS

Try taking slow, deep breaths. With each breath feel yourself relaxing. Allow each breath to bring you deeper inside yourself.

Imagine your breath as a circle. Follow the circle for several minutes. You will find yourself quieting as you focus on following the circle.

Use meditating or yoga techniques you already know or music that quiets you.

V. THE BUS

The Bus and The Room are two exercises for exploring subpersonalities. They are designed to help you get acquainted and "see" your parts.

Center ... Place yourself, in your imagination, in a meadow. This meadow is a very safe place. If you feel any unease, remember that in imagery you can have whatever you need. Give yourself any object or person that you need to feel completely comfortable and safe ... Be aware of what you see in the meadow, the colors, background, foreground ... Notice the ground beneath your feet and the feeling of the breeze against your cheek or your hair ... Hear the birds singing and the trees rustling ... As you enjoy the beautiful meadow, you notice that there is a country lane running along side it. You notice in the far distance a bus approaching. When you first see it, it is only a speck but as it approaches you become aware of its size and features... The bus pulls up along side your meadow, the door opens and the parts of yourself emerge. Stand back and watch as they get off the bus and enter the meadow. Just be aware of them for now. Notice who is there and where they go .... Then step up onto the steps of the bus and look inside ... Who is driving the bus? ... Who is left on the bus? ... Does the part(s) that is still on the bus need some attention? If you choose, you can get on the bus and talk to that part. You might want to encourage it to come out or ask what it needs ... Return to the meadow. Look around ... Is there a part you would like to know better? ... Where is it in the meadow? ... Who is it near? ... If you would like, approach that part. Notice how it is dressed, how it stands, how old it is. Ask it to talk to you. Ask any questions you would like ...

Now it is time to leave the meadow. Say good-bye ... Be aware that you can come back here anytime you would like. You can come back to finish a conversation, to observe more, to get to know other parts. But now it is time to come back. Bring your attention back to yourself sitting in the chair ... to the sounds in the room where you are ... to your body being supported by the chair. And when you are ready, gently open your eyes.

Take notes in your journal about this experience.

Good Questions:

1. Who was left on the bus? How old is this part? Why did this part stay behind?

2. Who was driving the bus?

3. Were you aware of how the parts grouped themselves when they got off?

4. Who do you feel curious about?

VI. THE ROOM

Take a few moments to bring yourself to center ... Affirm your choice to let whatever needs to happen to happen ... Imagine yourself in a pleasant room. It is a safe place, perhaps a room you know or one you construct right now in your image ... Be aware of the size of the room ... the furniture in it ... the doors and windows ... the temperature ... Adjust anything that makes you feel uneasy so that you know you are safe ... Then approach one of the doors of the room ... Open the door and stand back to watch your subpersonalities enter ... Allow them to come into the room. Look around ... Notice who is here ... Notice how they are dressed ... their ages ... their postures ... Notice how the parts arrange themselves in relationship to each other ... Choose one part and walk up to it ... Ask it if it will talk to you ... Ask what role it plays in your life ... Ask what it wants ... what it needs ... Does it get enough air time? ... What would it do if it had more? ... less? ... Ask the part any questions you would like about what is going on in your life or decisions you need to make ... Remember to keep your questions appropriate to the age and role of the part. Accept its answers ... Thank it for talking to you. Say good-bye. You may choose to talk to another part or to leave the room for now. When you do leave, be aware that you can return at any time to continue meeting and conversing with your parts ... Return yourself to the chair you are sitting in, aware of the sounds around you ... the feeling of your real room. Open your eyes and record in your journal the experience you have just had.

VII. THE PIE

This exercise uses what you have learned in the above two. You can use a page in your journal or a separate sheet of paper. You may want to use a large piece of drawing paper or newsprint. Make a circle that fills most of the page. In the center, make a small circle (on 81/2 x 11 paper I'd make the center circle about 1" in diameter). Now divide the circle into pie sections. Take a moment to reconnect to the parts you saw in The Bus or The Room or ones you have identified in other ways. In each piece of the pie, draw a part or a symbol that represents that part. I suggest using color—crayons, oil crayons, colored pencils, markers, paints. Trust that what shows up is what is supposed to be there. Leave one pie piece blank to indicate that there are still unidentified parts.

VIII. THE ART JOURNAL

Art journaling is a technique that I have recently learned and found very effective. If you want to get the full scoop on how to do this, you may want to contact an art therapist. Sometimes they run groups or have single day workshops where you can learn this and other art therapy techniques. We're going to focus on using the art journal for expanding your knowledge of the sub-personalities.

You can use the pages of the journal you have been using for dialogue to do this. Or you may want to select a different notebook that is larger or has other features (like unlined pages, or heavier ones). It is permissible to use any art media that appeals to you. You can draw, paint with water colors, use oil crayons, colored pencils, markers. If you like to draw or paint or whatever, this is the time to let your creative spirit go. If you are an artist, do whatever occurs to you to get better in touch with your subpersonalities. If you are not an artist (like me!), I would suggest choosing the medium that you like best and sticking with it.

When I started working in an art journal, I was introduced to the idea of using collage so that is what I did. It is the easiest for me—no drawing required. But I also do have drawings of my major subpersonalities and in my journal I pasted marker drawings for many of them. If you want to collage, gather a bunch of old magazines. I got National Geographics from my daughter because they have such marvelous pictures. I also collected popular magazines from my hair dresser (hair dressers always keep a supply of new ones and have to discard the old).

Now choose the first subpersonality to work on and go through the magazines looking for words and pictures that jump out at you. Don't think too much about this. Let your creative self have the floor. When you have snipped and/or torn a pile, begin assembling them. I made my pages multi-layered and liked that effect. You keep lifting a picture or word to find another, gradually uncovering more and more facets of the part.

You can also use the other materials, painting, markers etc. and do the same thing. Don't think a lot. Just get images, colors, shapes, on paper that seem to represent your part.

When you think you are done, choose one picture or section of the work and try to dialogue with that. It is very interesting after doing the art work to dialogue with an image or even the part. It enriches your dialogue and further fleshes out the subpersonality.

IX. CHOOSING A THERAPIST

Since I have mentioned quite a few times in the text of this book that working with a therapist is a good idea, I thought perhaps we should talk more about that. First I want to make it clear what it means to work with a therapist. If you have never done this, you may think only people who are mentally ill or who have really screwed up their lives (or their marriages, or their kids!!) go to therapy. There probably was a time when that was true. But today many people seek therapy because they want to live their lives better—not because they have screwed them up. They want to learn more about what makes them tick and find ways to get more of what they want in their relationships and/or their work.

As a therapist, I consider it my responsibility to do my own therapeutic work. The better I get at being a therapist, the more challenges I meet and the more I need to be in therapy! My dear friend and mentor Betty Bosdell (remember her from the preface?) used to say, "All of our stuff is all of our stuff." I think she meant that we are always learning about ourselves when other people share themselves with us. So as a therapist this is an occupational hazard (and joy and reward!). She also meant we shouldn't be so worried about sharing and looking foolish. The more honest we are in sharing ourselves with others, the more we learn that we have a lot in common!

So if you have never been in therapy but have been wondering if you need to be or thinking that you want to be, congratulations— you have a great adventure ahead of you.

Where to start? The Internet provides a number of resources. So does your phone book. You can find lists under headings such as Counselors, Marriage and Family Therapists, Psychologists, Social Workers. In the medical doctor category are psychiatrists. Some of them do therapy but many do evaluations and prescribe medications (like anti-anxiety and anti-depressant drugs). If you have any doubt about whether you need medication, ask your doctor for a referral to a psychiatrist for an evaluation. Often the psychiatrist will refer you to someone else for therapy if together you decide that is what you need (in addition to or instead of medication).

Most states license master degreed therapists. Check to see if your state does. (My state of Illinois has the State Department of Regulation that provides licenses to plumbers, hairdressers, and therapists! One can call that department for a list of professions that are licensed.) If so, the qualified ones will be licensed and you will want to look for that. If there is no licensing for master level therapists, you do want to be sure the one you choose has a master's degree in social work, counseling, marital and family therapy, or psychology. It gets confusing because when you talk to someone trained in one discipline they may think their kind of training is the best. But a secret all of us in the field know is that if the schools are accredited and reputable, the quality of their training is pretty comparable.

There are also therapists who have doctorates in clinical psychology (Ph.D.), psychology (Psy.D.), counseling, marriage and family therapy (Ed.D. or Ph.D. depending on the school).

There is a Psychosynthesis Directory. Of course someone trained in psychosynthesis is going to know what you are talking about when you start talking about parts. Therapists trained in Jungian analysis will also be familiar with this way of thinking.

There is probably a Mental Health Center and/or a Family Service Center in your area. The phone book is a good place to find them. They often have less intimidating names and are listed under the heading "Counseling or Psychology." These agencies usually have a sliding scale based on your income. They receive funds from the state and/or federal government. You will want to ask where they get their funds and who has access to your records. Also ask about credentials, supervision of staff, and accreditation. Excellent therapists often work in agencies so don't think you will be getting second best.

Ask you doctor and your friends if they know good therapists in your area. Don't underestimate the value of "word of mouth." A satisfied customer is always a good source of where to get good service.

After you know the credentials are good, talk to the person you will be seeing. Do a phone interview first. Ask about their style, their training, and do they know about parts models. Whether or not they work with subpersonalities matters a lot if you want them to help you with the work in this book. But if your concerns are not directly related to parts work, it is probably not the number one criterion. The number one criterion is: Do you feel comfortable talking to this person? If you hit it off, it will probably work. If you feel your personalities aren't a good match, or you feel talked down to or patronized, it almost certainly will not work. Research shows that the relationship between the client and the therapist is the most significant factor related to success. Choosing a therapist is almost like choosing a spouse. It may not make a lot of logical sense but it had better "feel" right! If ever there was a time to trust your gut, this is it!

When you set up the first appointment, make it clear you want to see whether this is a good fit for you. That will make it easier to say it doesn't feel quite right if it doesn't. Of course, we therapists are only human and we have self-esteem issues like everyone else. We would always rather be chosen than rejected. But most of us understand this thing about a good fit pretty well and are willing to accept your choice without being too hurt. Your job is not to keep the therapist from having hurt feelings. Your job is to look after you and choose someone with whom you feel comfortable. Ask all the questions you have. Make a list if you need to. The way your questions are handled will help you get a "feel" for this person.

I believe we grow best from a feeling of safety. You should feel safe with the person you have chosen for a therapist. If you do not feel safe, find someone else! It doesn't matter whether there is anything "real" to be afraid of. You don't have to explain your feelings. Just take care of yourself.

X. MORE SAMPLE DIALOGUES

[A dialogue written at 4:35 a.m., awake and staving off a sense of panic that sometimes comes in the night, a feeling of not being able to breathe and needing to get up. This feeling has been traced to the two youngest talking parts, Jeanie and Jeanie II.]

#1 Purpose: To identify the needs of the young parts who seem to wake me up.

J: *Anybody need to talk?*

Jn (Jeanie): *I guess me.*

J: *What, honey?*

Jn: *I don't know really. I hate being awake when you are sup-*

posed to be sleeping.

J: *Yeah, me too.*

Jn: *It always makes me feel lonely and scared.*

J: *Yes, sweetie. But I am here for you. I won't leave you.*

Jn: *She did you know.*

JnII (Jeanie II): *Yeah!*

J: *I know. I know guys. I know there is no understanding that from your point of view.* [Note: this is about my mother leaving me with an aunt when I was 18 months old. It is important not to make excuses even though, as an adult, I know there was a good reason for her leaving—my dad was being shipped out to go to World War II and she wanted to be with him as long as she could. She was gone for 6 weeks and it made a difference for me. But now I wouldn't have wanted her to make any other choice. The young parts are not interested in excuses or reasons. They just want to be understood.]

Jn: *Maybe I sort of get it but it doesn't help. It just makes me feel greedy and selfish to want her so much and to feel so abandoned.*

J: *Oh honey, you are not greedy and selfish. You are just little and that is how it is. When you are little, all you want is to know Mommy is always there.*

Jn: *Yes.*

JnII: *Yeah!*

J: *I am sorry she had to leave you. But I never will.*

Jn. & JnII: *How can you promise?*

J: *Because we are all one, all together. And I know you need me* *to pay attention. I won't forget that. So I can't really leave you.*

Jn: *You can forget us.*

J: *Yes. I can but I am determined not to. I guess when I feel the panic; I'll always know you two are there.*

Jn. & JnII: *Yes!*

J: *If I try to pay attention more, will you cut out the panic episodes?*

Jn: *Only if I'm not scared.*

J: *OK. I'll try to help you not be scared. Can you find another way to tell me?*

Jn: *You have to see me, recognize I'm there.*

J: *Yes. And that is hard I guess unless I feel panic or scared.*

Jn: *You could just remember me when you wake up and cuddle me and stroke me and tell me it is all OK.*

J: *Yes, Baby. I can do that. And I'll really try to do it on a regular basis.*

JnII: *Or we can always remind you...*

J: *Yes. You've certainly showed me that you can.*

Jn: *Are you mad?*

J: *No. I'm not. Really. I just like/need to sleep.*

Jn: *So do we.*

J: *OK. Let's go do it. We have an hour and it will feel good.*

BOTH: *OK!*

[Note: This dialogue pretty much ended the panic episodes. Now if I wake up suddenly, I get up and write a few minutes to Jeanie and that takes care of it.]

#2 Purpose: To check in with the parts.

J: *Anyone want to speak?*

Jn: *Just say you love me.*

J: *I do. I love you, Jeanie. You do not have be afraid—or spur a panic to get my attention. Here I am and I love you.*

Jn: *I like it when we play. I like it when you adore C (grand-child).*

J: *Good. I am trying to give you some space.*

Jn: *When we get home can we play in the art journal again?*

J: *Of course. I was thinking about having my table cleared and lots of space to do that. It will be cool!*

Jn: *Can we paint, too?*

J: *Yes! Yes. I can hardly wait!*

Jn: *Me too.*

J: *One day at a time, Baby, one day at a time.*

Jn: *OK. Let's sleep!*

#3 Purpose: To try to find out what keeps me from cleaning up a disaster of a room in my house. I really want it cleaned up so I can move to a different room but I can't seem to get it together.

J: *Who needs to speak about this issue of messiness?*

CO (Commanding Officer): *Me.*

SB (JnII. I used to call her Spoiled Brat. That didn't go over

so well with her!) *ME!!*

SL (Sophisticated Lady): *Me.*

MM (Maskless Me): *Me!*

J: *Ok. Who begins?*

CO: *I am the one for whom this is an obvious issue. I'm the white gloved inspector and I have issues with the messes.*

J: *Yes. I know you do. Tell me about that.*

CO: *I guess I started criticizing you for this when you were about ten and Mother yelled at you and even punished you for your messy room.*

J: *I remember the punishment but you know, I don't remember her yelling. But she says she did.*

CO: *She did.*

J: *You know this?*

CO: *It is where I learned.*

J: *Oh. That makes sense.*

CO: *I like order. It makes me feel in control. I like to do the ordering. I wish you'd let me out more. I like to sort, pitch, straighten.*

J: *Yes. I wish y you were out more, too.*

JnII: *Wait a minute!*

J: *Yes. You have something to say here, I take it?*

JnII: *Don't be nasty to me.*

J: *No. I'm sorry. I didn't mean to. I guess I figure you make the messes.*

JnII: *So?*

J: *You are snippy.*

JnII: *Yeah? So?*

J: *Let's work together. I want to hear what you have to say about this.*

JnII: *Well, for one thing I don't want him running things.*

J: *Because?*

JnII: *Because he is a prick! He wants everything so perfect and he bitches all day about it. He puts us all down and calls us a slob.*

CO: *She is the slob.*

JnII: *I am not! I just don't wanna take orders from him.*

CO: *Yuk!*

J: *Let's not mud sling here guys.*

JnII: *Yeah.*

CO: *Okay but don't give her too much energy.*

J: *I want to hear her out. Jeanie II what was it when we were a kid that made you rebel and not want to clean up?*

JnII: *I heard your mom always fretting about the work she had to do. It seemed like it made her feel bad about herself even though I never heard Daddy nag.*

J: *I don't think he did. But maybe her dad or mom did.*

JnII: *Maybe. Anyway she scared me. It felt like a bad thing to have to work hard to clean and make things nice. It felt like there was punishment out there for not doing it.*

J: *So. I think we needed K to be critical to provide that.*

JnII: *Maybe. I don't get all that stuff too much. I just know it made me scared of being a grown up and of doing housework types of stuff. Sort of like if my mommy couldn't get it right, how could I ever? So it would be better not to do it at all, ever.*

J: *Wow, JnII that is a mouthful! But what about the issue of being rebellious? It has that feel to it.*

JnII: *That came a little older. I'm not sure I'm the one who can tell you why. I am not the one who felt angry and rebellious.*

F (Fury): *Maybe it is because I never get to come out!! I was always being squelched.*

J: *Aha. You again, Fury!*

F: *Again?*

J: *Well, I was just reading and typing one of your dialogues yesterday.*

F: *Yeah but that was written way back.*

J: *I know. So what is it now?*

F: *Just that I was always squelched.*

JnII: *So I acted out in more passive-aggressive ways.*

J: *Ah. So that is what you were doing!*

JnII: *Yes. I would rather have seen Fury howl!*

J: *Scary to me!*

F: *Scaredy Cat! You were always afraid of everything.*

J: *I think I learned that anger, especially, was scary. I don't remember any tantrums but I did pout.*

JnII: *Yep. That was me!*

F: *But I wanted to let her rip!*

JnII: *And I wanted you to.*

J: *Wow! What would that have looked like?*

F: *Oh, you know—just your standard run of the mill tantrum! Yell. Kick my feet. Throw myself down. Refuse to be calmed till I'm good and ready.*

J: *You and A. And C. And S!*

F: *They have the right idea.*

J: *Who kept that from happening?*

CL (Chicken Little): *The sky is falling.*

J: *Oh, you?*

CL: *Well, really the sky would fall, surely!*

J: *Or not.*

Jn (Jeanie): *I didn't want it to happen either.*

J: *Oh, Honey. Hi.*

Jn: *Hi.*

JnII: *How come you always greet her so nice?*

J: *Did I greet you not nice today?*

JnII: *I guess you were okay.*

J: *Then stop grousing.*

JnII: *See. You always shut me up.*

J: *I'm sorry you feel that way. I am trying to listen.*

Jn: *Well, I want a turn.*

J: *Okay, Baby. It is your turn.*

Jn: *I just feel scared when people get angry. I didn't like Mommy to be mad. Or upset about cleaning. It seemed like cleaning should be fun. I thought playing in the water while cleaning the bathroom was the best. I don't know why Mommy didn't like to clean stuff. My favorite was anything that needed water. And soapy stuff.*

J: *Well, next time I need to clean something, I'll let you.*

Jn: *Yeah. That's fun. And I like it that John said maybe that is a way we can feel close to Mommy.*

J: *Yes. But how about you, JnII?*

JnII: *Yeah? What about me?*

J: *Well, this cleaning issue?*

JnII: *Don't like it. Mama didn't like it. I don't like it. Don't plan to do much of it!*

J: *But why the rebellion?*

JnII: *I just didn't wanna fail is all.*

J: *Oh. Fail, eh?*

JnII: *Yeah fail, OK?*

J: *I can see how failure gets into this. And maybe your momma had to do too much cleaning as a kid. She was the oldest of four girls and her mom cleaned people's houses. She probably had to help a lot.*

CO: *Can we get on with the real issue?*

J: *Which is?*

CO: *Getting organized. Why can't we quit this drivel and go DO something!!*

J: *I guess we can. I am about to fall asleep sitting up, writing!*

CO: *Well, let's go do some work. We've examined how everyone feels about it long enough. We need to work.*

J: *Yeah. Maybe. But I want everyone to know I appreciate your forthrightness. It is helpful to know all this. I'm not sure it helped resolve anything but we'll see. And we can always come back to it.*

All: *Yeah!*

[Note: On this very day I started working on that room—did 2-3 hours and kept plugging away till it was done! I have not become a neatnik but I feel less rebellious about cleaning up and do more of it.]

REFERENCE SECTION
(for that nagging part that wants to KNOW)

PSYCHOSYNTHESIS

Assagioli, Roberto. *Psychosynthesis, A Manual of Principles and Techniques*. Penguin Books Ltd. Harmondsworth, Middlesex, England, 1977.

> This innocent looking little book is a collection of Roberto Assagioli's writings on his theory of psychosynthesis. When it was required reading in my first class, I slogged through it. I find it a bit heavy going but if you really want to read "the source" straight from THE horse's mouth, this is it! It is also interesting and thought provoking. And it has great ideas for therapists to use in their work.

Assagioli, Roberto. *The Act of Will*. Penguin Books Ltc. Harmondsworth, Middlesex, England, 1973.

> Concise and clear, this Assagioli offering you will find easier to read. It explains his theory about The Will and if that is interesting to you, this book will clear up any questions.

Ferrucci, Piero. *What we May Be, Techniques for Psychological and Spiritual Growth*. J.P. Tarcher, Inc. Los Angeles, CA. 1982.

> If you want to understand the theory of psychosynthesis and do some personal growth work to make it all come alive for you, this book is the ticket. I always use it as a text when I teach psychosynthesis because it explains Assagioli so well. Therapists love it because they can use the exercises with their clients.

King, Vivian. *Being Here When I Need Me, An Inner Journey.* Inner Way Productions, Forres Scotland. 1998.

> Dr. King is a psychosynthesis practitioner. I heard her present her ideas about using guided imagery for personal physical healing many years ago and have used them many times. This is her guide to using the techniques of psychosynthesis for personal growth.

Parfitt, Will. *The Elements of Psychosynthesis.* Element Books Ltd. Longmead, Shaftesbury, Dorset, England. 1990.

> Used as a secondary text in teaching psychosynthesis at the graduate level, this is a nice description of the theory with some exercises to help you make it your own.

VOICE DIALOGUE

Stone, Hal. Stone, Sidra.

Embracing Ourselves.

> Voice Dialogue is the parts model on which much of my work is based (after Assagioli's concept of subpersonalities). This is the manual for Voice Dialogue. If you really want to understand the idea about parts of the personality, this is the original source for talking to your parts in the ways I have described. Read the Stones and if you ever hear they are presenting, go to see them.

Embracing Each other, Relationship as Teacher, Healer & Guide.

> Expand your understanding of the parts model, Voice Dialogue, with this exciting book about how we relate through our parts to the parts of others.

Embracing Your Inner Critic.

I told you Hal wrote a whole book about this guy! I'm not sure if the book is still attainable but I know he has some of it on tape. If you are struggling with your Critic and not getting anywhere, pursue this avenue to better understanding how it works and how you can get a dialogue going with this essential (but sometimes pesky) element of your personality.

Partnering, A New Kind of Relationship: How to Love Each Other Without Losing Yourselves.

Voice Dialogue applied to your primary relationship.

The Shadow King.

Sidra's book about the inner patriarch! Wonderful reading for both women "and the men who love them." Sidra dispenses with blaming the "other sex" for the oppression of women in our culture and gets to the heart of it—internalized concepts of the patriarchy and women's roles passed down from one generation of women to the next.

The Stone's books and tapes are available through:

New World Library
14 Pamaron Way
Novato, CA 94949
800.972.6657

OTHER REALLY GREAT READS

Baldwin, Christina. *One to One: Self-Understanding through Journal Writing.* M. Evans and Company, New York. 1977.

This is the book that got me started on journaling years ago. It will help you expand journaling beyond dialogue.

Cameron, Julia. *The Artist's Way: A Spiritual Path to Higher Creativity.* G. P. Putnam's Sons, New York. 1992.

> I give Julia and her book credit for getting me started on writing. It will help you meet and use your creative part. Even if you don't think you have such a part or have no desire to do any art form, I think you could benefit. She is the source of the morning pages idea for journaling. And she has you go on special dates with yourself that are super!

Jung, C.G. *Archetypes of the Collective Unconscious, Collected Works.* Vol. 9, par. 1-86.

> [Anything by or about Jung is worth exploring. His work is compatible with Assagioli's.] If you want to go deeper into theory, Jung is a fascinating trip. Hal and Sidra Stone are Jungian therapists as is Ira Progoff (whose book is next!) Jung talks about archetypes (like the Warrior and the Earth Mother, for example—parts that are universal) and you will see the relationship to subpersonalities here.

Progoff, Ira. *At a Journal Workshop: The Basic Text and Guide for Using the* Intensive Journal. Dialogue House Library, New York. 1975.

> Progoff uses lots of imagery and a different form of dialogue that is very useful. Jungian training facilities often offer classes in his form of journal work. I was lucky enough to attend a four day advanced workshop lead by the master himself at DePaul University some years ago (more years than I care to count so I don't know that Progoff is still teaching.)

Rainwater, Janette. *You're in Charge: A Guide to Becoming your own Therapist.* Guild of Tutors Press, Los Angeles. 1979.

> This is a great little work book with lots of imagery and creative ways to do personal work from a psychosynthesis perspective. Don't succumb to the siren's call of the sub title though. There is no substitute for the real thing when you need a therapist. All of this stuff is doing your own therapeutic work.

Schwartz, Richard C. *Internal Family Systems.* Guilford Press, New York. 1995.

> Schwartz uses the paradigm of family systems to conceptualize his parts model. Therapists who have not read his work will find it particularly interesting. If you want to explore how your parts operate a lot like a family does, this book will give you the framework to do that.

Note: Many of these titles are old and you might find them out of print. There is a way to order out of print books on the Internet, check it out.

ACKNOWLEDGMENTS

Saying, "Thank you" is the fun part of writing a book. But it is also a hard part. There are so many people I want to acknowledge and "thank you" seems so little to say about their contributions.

My daughter Sandra Moustafa was one of my earliest readers. She read to give me the view point of a person uninitiated to the ideas and the language I was introducing. She read the rewrites and the final version. Her insights and suggestions were invaluable. Together we painstakingly worked on the placement of the illustrations. And at every turn she praised my work and encouraged me. Sandra did all of this while being "mother extraordinaire" to her four children.

Posthumously, I thank and honor my dear friend Naomi Rubin. Naomi loved the written language and was thrilled that I had finally begun to write. On a lunch date, she heard the first page— the page I scrambled to get done that morning! I read it to her because her eyesight was beginning to fail. But her mind was as sharp as ever. When I considered aloud whether to include the theoretical material, it was Naomi who asked, "Why don't you talk about the academic part of the reader and the part that needs to just let go and do it?" I missed her wonderful store of grammatical knowledge as I struggled with the final editing; often wishing I could pick up the phone to get her take on a decision.

Naomi, Helen Haugsnes, and I spent many delightful moments reviewing the progress of my book. In one such session, I bemoaned my unsuccessful attempts to find an illustrator. Suddenly Helen said, "I know who you need. It is Susu!" Susu turned out to be the wonderful Susan Breck Smith whose work delights me.

Helen took her task as a "reader" very seriously and had ideas for improvements thought of by no one else. I am deeply grateful for her encouragement in this and many of my endeavors over our long friendship. In addition, Helen introduced me to her sister Eva Bundenthal, who was one of the first people to read an early draft. Eva was new to the idea of subpersonalities and her suggestions about how to describe this concept were invaluable.

My Abundia sisters deserve my deepest gratitude for their belief in my project and in me. Barbara Spaulding was an enthusiastic cheerleader. Cheri Erdman gave above and beyond the call of friendship in her thorough editing and suggestions. Sally Strosahl had creative ideas and also went over the text with a fine-tooth comb. I am grateful to her for allowing me to use her personal story to illustrate a point. Susan Ross caught subtle errors. To these four I owe much for continuing love and encouragement.

Mary Shesgreen and Maureen McKane from my consultation group read and had valuable clinical input as the fine therapists they both are. Maureen also contributed her expertise as a writer.

I much appreciate the reading and comments given by Scott Zagurski. Scott told me he loved "self help" books and would be glad to read mine and give me feedback. His most delightful comment was, "This is not like any other self-help book I have ever read!" But he encouraged me nonetheless.

P.J. Hruby, my friend and student and teacher, gave the reader's copy her most serious attention. She had excellent advice about the structure and many helpful comments about the technical aspects of the work.

John Hofstra and Caroline Conger, two of my most valued teachers, each said, "I love it!" That goes a long, long way for me.

Melissa Wilke graciously contributed her subpersonality map so that my readers would see an original way of displaying their parts. I am grateful to her for her willingness to share her "self."

Susan Breck Smith, Helen's Susu, was a paragon of patience and encouragement. I have made a new friend through e-mail, phone conversations and the charm of the characters she has created. Nina Davis gently nudged me along as we worked on the formatting and final copy. Without the expertise of these two, I would have been lost in the fog, unable to find my way to a polished finished product.

My beloved family: daughters and their husbands Sandra and Ehab, Michelle and Jay; grandchildren Jessica, Alex, Micaela, Courtney, Adam, Dalya, and Johnathon; cousins Joe and Lorraine Gore—all had a part. They believed in me. They provided encouragement and laughter and love.

Last but far from least my great thanks to my long-suffering and much-loved husband, Ken. He is my rock. I could not have done any of the parts of this project without him. But especially I could not have done the computer gymnastics! He is a whiz and was always willing to take time from his own work to sort me out. His love and support, above all, are treasured.

Jeanette C. Zweifel
Naperville, Illinois
Fall, 2002

INDEX

Share *Will the Real Me Please Stand Up?* with friends, colleagues, clients!

Book Order Form

Number of copies (at $15.00 per copy) _____   Total _____

(Special price for therapists ordering 5 or more copies–$13.00 plus shipping and handling.)

Shipping and handling, add $5.00 per copy _____

My check or money order for _____ is enclosed.

Name _____

Organization (if applicable) _____

Address _____

City, State, Zip _____

Phone (_____)_____E-mail_____

Please make your check payable to: Jeanette C. Zweifel. Return to:

Jeanette C. Zweifel
C/O Nell Thurber Press
61 Swift Lane
Naperville, IL 60565
Phone:630.355.3367